MOVING
FORWARD
FASTER

D0743304

The Mental Evolution from
Fake Lean to REAL Lean

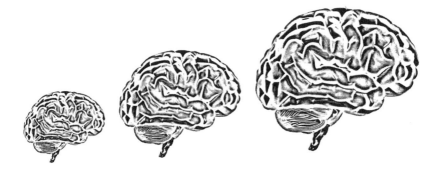

Bob Emiliani

The CLBM, LLC
Wethersfield, CT
Tel: 860.558.7367   www.bobemiliani.com

Cover design and page layout by Tom Bittel, bittelworks@sbcglobal.net
www.dadsnoisybasement.com

Library of Congress Control Number: 2010913050

Emiliani, M.L., 1958–

        Moving Forward Faster: The Mental Evolution from
        Fake Lean to REAL Lean
        / M.L. Emiliani

Includes bibliographical references and index
1. Business   2. Lean management   3. Leadership

I. Title
ISBN-13: 978-0-9845400-1-3

First Edition   January 2011

Ordering information: www.bobemiliani.com

Disclaimer: This book is produced with the wholesome intent to improve the practice of management, with specific interest in moving from conventional zero-sum, power-based bargaining, sellers' market view to non-zero-sum, collaborative problem identification and correction, buyers' market view. Reasonable efforts have been made to insure the accuracy and utility of the information contained in this workbook. User accepts full responsibility for any misunderstandings, misinterpretations, or misapplications of content made by user. No warranties or representations as to the accuracy, completeness, timeliness, non-infringement, or fitness for any particular purpose of the information given. In no event will any liability be accepted from any party for damages, whether direct, indirect, special, consequential, punitive or other for any use or inability to use this workbook, including, but not limited to any damages for loss of profits, business interruption, or similar or related undesirable outcomes. User accepts responsibility for any and all results.

Made in the U.S.A. using print-on-demand technology.

Books by M.L. "Bob" Emiliani

Better Thinking, Better Results: Case Study and Analysis of an Enterprise-Wide Lean Transformation

Practical Lean Leadership: A Strategic Leadership Guide for Executives

REAL LEAN: Understanding the Lean Management System (Volume One)

REAL LEAN: Critical Issues and Opportunities in Lean Management (Volume Two)

REAL LEAN: The Keys to Sustaining Lean Management (Volume Three)

REAL LEAN: Learning the Craft of Lean Management (Volume Four)

REAL LEAN: Strategies for Lean Management Success (Volume Five)

REAL LEAN: Unsolved Problems in Lean Management (Volume Six)

Principles of Mass and Flow Production by F.G. Woollard with Bob Emiliani, 55th Anniversary Special Reprint Edition

Zen master Kakumei said to his student:

"You will know Lean when you know nothing."

Preface

After many years of experience with Lean management, it has become apparent to me that how executives comprehend business is a major impediment to understanding Lean management – but not in the usual ways that people think of: leadership, production, accounting, process improvement, etc. Instead, my interest is in the numerous economic, social, political, and historical aspects of Lean management that very few people have ever thought about, and how these can provide a much better explanation for the overall lack of Lean success despite many decades of effort. Strong, noteworthy Lean transformations remain few in number, and we can expect more of the same if the path that we are on remains unchanged.

The economic, social, political, and historical aspects of Lean management are akin to the basic mathematical operators, + - × ÷. By way of metaphor, it seems that we have been teaching a higher level math to executives who do not yet understand these four fundamental operators. We have been trying to teach algebra to people who do not first understand arithmetic. Value stream maps, set-up reduction, A3 reports, kaizen, kanban, visual controls, work cells, standardized work, takt time, one-piece flow, etc., are the equivalent of algebra. Managers (and workers) apply these without truly understanding why, principally because they do not yet understand the four fundamental operators: the economic, social, political, and historical aspects of Lean management.

People often characterize Lean management as "common sense." That perception has tripped up many people, and usually is accompanied by the view among executives that Lean is something that other people do. This book will inform readers in a very direct way, that, for most executives Lean management is not common sense, and that it is as much, if not more, for executives than anyone else.

The format of the chapters in this book is different: You will find a statement followed by short bullet points describing how the statement is inconsistent with Lean management. Each chapter presents the key economic, social, and **political** ideas that must diminish or be eliminated, and historical facts that must be understood and accepted in order to experience long-term success with Lean management. Based on my observations and research, these 85 items represent most of the fundamental knowledge that Lean practitioners lack yet must become aware of in order to succeed long-term. Doing so will remove barriers that inhibit flow in material and information processing.

The economic ideas are labeled E1 through E24; the social ideas are labeled S1 through S22; the political ideas are labeled P1 through P18; and the historical ideas are labeled H1 through H21. This labeling system allows individual executives or management teams to precisely pinpoint items they understand well or misunderstand, and the specific items that require further thought and study. Appendix III provides examples of simple spreadsheets and charts that can be used to precisely identify areas to work on.

Awareness of many of these 85 items would normally emerge over time, through executives' daily application of Lean principles and practices. The problem is that most executives do not apply Lean principles and practices. Instead, they simply "support" Lean and do not think and actually learn Lean management first-hand. Therefore, they never learn these 85 items, all of which are essential for Lean success.

This book delivers to readers in about 50 pages, and in a few hours of reading time, what a dedicated Lean thinker-practitioner might learn over a period of 15, 20, or 30 years. While some will consider this to be quite an accomplishment, it gives me many concerns.

For example, I worry that delivering this knowledge to executives, without them having gone through the personal pain and pleasure of learning for themselves, will create new problems. Generally, when new information is simply handed to people in powerful positions, rather than them having to figure it out for themselves, they will take a cavalier attitude and think that because they understand the words they also understand their meaning. This is a grave error.

The 85 items that you will learn about in this book are only the beginning, the + - × ÷ operators, not the conclusion of what you need to know about Lean management.

I expect readers will gain much practical information from this book. The question is, will executives actually apply this information and put the company on the path of REAL Lean - the application of both the "Continuous Improvement" and "Respect for People" principles? Will they mentally evolve from where they are today, or will they instead decide, once and for all, that they cannot accept REAL Lean and continue along with zero-sum Fake Lean? I certainly hope not, but such outcomes are far beyond my control.

I hope that this small book helps REAL Lean management move forward, faster, and yields overwhelmingly positive outcomes for people.

Bob Emiliani
November 2010
Wethersfield, Conn.

Fake Lean

Continuous Improvement

REAL Lean

Continuous Improvement **+** Respect for People

People = employees, suppliers, customers, investors, and communities

Key Point to Remember

Thinking of Lean management narrowly, as only continuous improvement, is a long out-dated perspective. REAL Lean management consists of two key principles, "Continuous Improvement" and "Respect for People." The "Respect for People" principle cannot be treated as optional. It is what enables continuous improvement to occur, every day.

CAUTION

Do not assume you know what the "Respect for People" principle means.

Contents

Introduction

Lean has evolved over decades into a comprehensive system of progressive management that every organization and its stakeholders could greatly benefit from if managers correctly understood and applied Lean principles and practices. The trouble is, more than 95 percent of organizations that try Lean management do it wrong. As a result, most achieve some short-term gains, typically at the expense of others, but fail to achieve long-term success. Their Lean transformation is over almost as soon as it started.

This book seeks to help correct these unfortunate outcomes by providing vital new information to executives. It is information that they might learn after decades of Lean management practice, distilled into a format that will make obvious the requirements for achieving long-term success.

What does "Lean transformation" mean? To most people it means an enterprise-wide Lean transformation in which all people in all departments of an organization consistently apply Lean principles and practices. It means to expand the application of Lean management beyond operations and into every internal business process. It also means to apply Lean to every external business process that touches key stakeholders such as suppliers, intermediate customers, end-use customers, investors, and communities.

What I mean by "Lean transformation" is enterprise-wide Lean transformation *plus* an evolutionary change in the mindset and thinking of senior managers. It means to transform the executive mind, over time, from being deeply rooted in conventional management to becoming a skilled Lean management thinker and practitioner.

The focus of this book is the Lean transformation of executive minds;

changing their beliefs, which then leads to changes in their behaviors and competencies. This greatly assists, if not completely enables, enterprise-wide Lean transformations, a topic has been covered in detail in my book, *Better Thinking, Better Results* (second edition, 2007). Please read it, because flow changes everything.

We know empirically that it is not sufficient to apply Lean principles and practices to all business processes; the minds of senior managers must evolve as well. It would be more accurate to say "total Lean transformation," where the word "total," then, means people (the top leaders) and processes, as well as preserving and improving this way of leading through future generations of managers.

Lean leadership training has long focused on Lean tools and, more recently, on changing leadership behaviors, but these approaches have not been successful at creating REAL Lean leaders (application of both the "Continuous Improvement" and "Respect for People" principles). The reasons why Lean management is not more common in business remains unrecognized, misunderstood, or ignored by those who develop and deliver Lean training to executives.

With this in mind, I thought it important to dig deep into the details and get to the heart of the matter. This effort is reflected in the *REAL LEAN* book series (2007-2010), which substantially explains why executives struggle with Lean and why Lean remains a niche management practice. The six books have received accolades, particularly among people who know Lean management very well. But, at over 1000 pages in total, it is doubtful that many executives will read all the books or be able to follow my lines of thinking regarding the key economic, social, **political**, and historical aspects of Lean management.

In this volume, I have triple-distilled the *REAL LEAN* book series.

This book contains four chapters that focus on the key economic, social, political, and historical aspects of Lean management. They show how and why Lean management is very difficult for executives to understand, particularly those who have practiced conventional management for 20 or 30 years. Lean management conflicts in ways large and small with almost everything that executives know and believe.

Success with Lean management requires certain economic, social, and political ideas to diminish in importance or be eliminated from the minds of executives. In addition, executives must become aware of the history of progressive management, which reveals a repetition of the same mistakes. These four categories are presented using an easy-to-read and comprehend format that will help executives clearly understand why they struggle with Lean.

Readers will begin to recognize that their economic, social, political, and historical inventories hide problems and impair their ability to understand Lean management. It explicitly presents the inventories that executives need to burn off in order to open up their minds to learn progressive REAL Lean management.

If executives can accept what is contained in these pages, they will evolve from 1911 view of Lean as zero-sum tools for efficiency, productivity, and cost-cutting to the 2011 and beyond view of Lean as a comprehensive, non-zero-sum, human-centered management system that is far superior to their current management practice.

Most senior managers I have met over the years believe they possess various special qualities and characteristics. What I have learned is that this clearly is not the case, and that having this perspective is a huge barrier to improving themselves and the organizations they lead. That, coupled with the cognitive dissonance that Lean management instantly creates, usually results in perpetuation of the status quo.

This book is meant to shake things up. It asks readers to question their basic beliefs about economics, social, political, and historical aspects of business, management, and leadership, and learn how these relate to their understanding and practice of Lean management. This book is provocative. It will challenge, annoy, frighten, enlighten, frustrate, educate, and enliven you. And, it will help executives move forward, faster.

Unlike other books that I have written, this volume does not contain detailed endnotes. This is a huge departure for me - the first ever in more than 30 years of writing - but it was done for the purpose of focusing your attention and keeping you locked on point. Readers who are interested in understanding the basis for the facts and arguments presented here should read the *REAL LEAN* book series, Volumes One through Six.

If executives can accept what they read here, they will possess a much deeper understanding of Lean management, and they will position themselves on a path to actually having a successful Lean transformation; a total Lean transformation.

• • • • •

Before we begin, I ask that you accept that each of the 85 items listed in Chapters 1 through 4 are categorized correctly (more or less). Disagreements over categorization are not necessary and will dilute the intended message. Please recognize that some of the items listed may cross categories.

Also, we must embrace a common understanding of Lean management to precisely establish the context of this book. The *Lean management system* is defined as:

> A non-zero-sum principle-based management system focused on creating value for end-use customers and eliminating waste, unevenness, and unreasonableness using the scientific method.

In *non-zero sum* business activities, all parties share in the gains (or losses); the so-called win-win. In contrast, zero-sum business activities are when one party gains at the expense of others (win-lose). *Zero-sum* is much more commonly found in business than non-zero-sum, despite the fact that it undercuts organizational capability-building and reduces long-term competitiveness.

The word *system* in the above definition of Lean management means:

> An organized and consistent set of principles and practices.

The Lean management system has two key principles:

> "Continuous Improvement"
> and
> "Respect for People"

I will refer to the application of both the "Continuous Improvement" and "Respect for People" principles as REAL Lean. Fake Lean means only the "Continuous Improvement" principle is put into practice.

"People" means the *stakeholders* in a narrow context, and also humanity in a larger context. The term *stakeholders* identify the five key groups of people that have long-term interests in an organization's success:

> Employees, suppliers, customers, investors, and communities.

Competitors can be important stakeholders as well.

To be successful with Lean management, executives must accept and practice the "Respect for People" principle. They must also accept the scientific method in their daily management practice for all business problems.

Finally, please be aware that the two major reasons why Lean transformations fail long-term are due to changes in company ownership and changes in leadership.

Invariably, new owners and new leaders replace Lean management with conventional management beliefs and practices. So you will have to make sure that new leaders know and believe what you know and believe about Lean management. You must teach your successors well for Lean to survive after you are gone.

Key Point to Remember

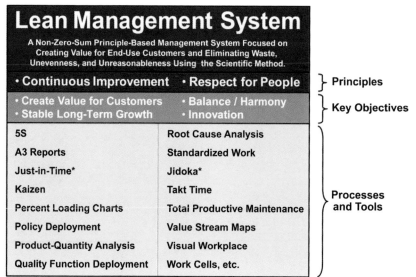

Lean Management System

A Non-Zero-Sum Principle-Based Management System Focused on Creating Value for End-Use Customers and Eliminating Waste, Unevenness, and Unreasonableness Using the Scientific Method.

• Continuous Improvement	• Respect for People	} Principles
• Create Value for Customers • Stable Long-Term Growth	• Balance / Harmony • Innovation	} Key Objectives

5S	Root Cause Analysis	
A3 Reports	Standardized Work	
Just-in-Time*	Jidoka*	
Kaizen	Takt Time	Processes and Tools
Percent Loading Charts	Total Productive Maintenance	
Policy Deployment	Value Stream Maps	
Product-Quantity Analysis	Visual Workplace	
Quality Function Deployment	Work Cells, etc.	

* TPS Principles

Lean management has long been widely misunderstood as "tools for the manager's toolkit," to drive internal operating performance. Lean is a management system designed for demand-driven buyers' markets (see Appendix I and II). It is the management system to use when competition is intense or likely to increase in intensity in the future.

CAUTION

Adopt Lean management for the benefit of your customers, to provide them with improved products and services, not for internal company reasons.

1

Economic Ideas That Must Diminish Or Be Eliminated

It is often assumed that economics is a pure science like mathematics or physics. Economics is, in fact, a social science. Therefore, it is not surprising that when a macro-economic problem arises, such as a major recession, one clique of economists says the problem was due to too much regulation, while another clique of economists says it was due to too little regulation, for example. You cannot rely on such faulty and divergent thinking to shape how you run your business.

Imagine a highway bridge that collapsed and caused many deaths and injuries. In the ensuing investigation, one engineering clique said bridge failure was due to overdesign and another engineering clique said it was due to under-design. The engineers will ignore facts, preferring to remain locked in argument rather than engaging in improvement. People will remain in harm's way, which is unacceptable. The field of engineering would never progress under such circumstances.

Various aspects of economics are almost meaningless when people studying the same problem come to vastly different conclusions on its causes. Please note that formal root cause analysis is never used by academic or industrial economists to discern the sources of failure. They simply make educated guesses at cause-and-effect, usually based on evidence that confirms their views.

Therefore, do not rely on your understanding of economics because it will likely misguide you. You will not evolve in your thinking and understanding of business as an executive if you do not question your canonical economic beliefs.

*Read this chapter as follows: A brief statement labeled
E1, E2, etc., represents an idea that is commonly held
by executives, in thought or action. This is followed
by short bullet points describing how the idea is
inconsistent with Lean management.*

———————

E1 - Shareholder supremacy.

• If shareholders rank supreme, then there is no way you can
actually be customer focused. You do not recognize the buyers'
market that your customers enjoy. This is a fundamental
leadership error.

• Shareholders are just one of several vital company stakeholders.
The others are employees, suppliers, customers, and communities.
All are needed for a business to function properly.

• Making shareholders (owners) supreme is a self-imposed
management decision, not a law or requirement.

• Shareholder supremacy will induce or force management to be
zero-sum in its decisions. People (employees, suppliers, etc.) will
then work against you.

• Shareholder supremacy undercuts teamwork.

• Shareholder supremacy is inconsistent with the "Respect for
People" principle because it favors one stakeholder over all others.

• All stakeholders must share in the gains and losses, not for one
stakeholder to gain at another's expense.

E2 - Shareholder is the customer.

• Shareholders are a stakeholder. Customer are the ones who pay
for, and usually use, the product or service.

• Shareholders can be customers when a company has an initial or
secondary public offering. Once shares trade to another party, the
new shareholder is no longer a customer, but they do obtain the
right to a portion of the wealth created - if you do a good job
satisfying cash-paying customers.

- Shareholders do not generate cash flow for company day-to-day. Only intermediate and end-use customers do that.
- Shareholders are important stakeholders whose interests management must strive to satisfy, in balance with the interests of other stakeholders.

E3 - Companies exist to maximize shareholder value.
- Three simple questions: Who told you this? How do you know it to be true? Where is the proof? No doubt you have accepted it on faith and never bothered to verify this claim for yourself. This idea is not fact-based, and therefore inconsistent with Lean thinking.
- If you do not satisfy the source of cash flow - customers - you're hurting your business and harming your shareholders.
- Maximizing shareholder value is a self-imposed management decision, not a law or requirement, and results in wasteful imbalances.
- In reality, it is impossible to maximize shareholder value. Shareholder Value = Corporate Value - Debt. Since debt is never zero, shareholder value cannot be maximized.
- Maximizing shareholder value (or "maximizing profits") is not a good corporate purpose because it is not one that all employees can rally around. Shareholder value and profits are very important - the reward for satisfying customers - but not the reason for existence.
- Corporate purpose should be to satisfy customer needs, and in doing so create shareholder value.
- Maximizing shareholder value is inconsistent with the "Respect for People" principle because it forces management to be zero-sum. People (employees, suppliers, etc.) will then work against you.
- As a result of trying to maximize shareholder value, you will under-fund new product development, R&D, or operations, and surely get into trouble.
- Stock price is important, but not the driver for execution.

E4 - Rational self-interested maximizer.

- Some people may be rational self-interested maximizers, but not all are. In fact, most are not.
- Thinking that self or other are rational self-interested maximizers will force management to be zero-sum. People (employees, suppliers, etc.) will then work against you.
- Generally, maximizing some item, "x," means minimizing other items, "y" and "z." Doing this will almost always get you into trouble.

E5 - Invisible hand.

- Adam Smith, in *The Wealth of Nations* (1776), did not say that self-interest *always* promotes the interests of society. Self-interest gone mad (e.g. greed, hoarding) is freed from the "invisible hand" and does not promote the interests of society.
- Smith stated the special case of small business (e.g. butcher, brewer, baker), where self-interest frequently promote the interests of society, not large businesses (disliked by Smith) or the general case of all businesses.
- If (mistakenly) comprehended by economists and executives as an axiom, that self-interest promotes the interests of society, then that is an illogical argument because the antecedent, "self- interest," does not necessarily lead to the consequent, "promotes the interests of society." For it to be seen as logical, one must deny the antecedent; i.e., benevolence does not promote the interests of society.
- Belief in the "invisible hand" ignores human intentionality, including efforts, ranging from simple to elaborate, to cheat or game a micro- or macro-economy. With this belief, you will assume various factors are out of your control when that may not actually be the case, or you may ignore empirical evidence.
- Mentioned only once in passing in *The Wealth of Nations* (1776), for the special case of small businesses, the "invisible hand" should not be a central feature of executives' economic thinking or decision-making.

E6 - Efficient markets.

- Efficient market hypothesis is not fact-based. It is a wish, not reality, due to pervasive information asymmetries in markets.

- Depression, recession, business cycles, bullwhip effect, national inventory turns = 8, current state value stream maps, fraud, unethical business behaviors, corrective actions that do not address root causes, etc., are empirical evidence of gross market inefficiency.

- Batch-and-queue (B&Q) material and information processing in supply chains are inefficient markets because they maximize the consumption of resources.

E7 - Free market fundamentalism.

- Free markets are a fine concept, but in practice some rules for markets are needed just as rules are need for roadways and the home.

- Basic rules, and occasionally complex rules, are pragmatic and necessary to avoid bad, expensive outcomes, as well as repetition of unfavorable outcomes.

- "Economic freedom" must be bounded so as not to be used by the powerful as a license to externalize costs, avoid accountability, or cheat.

E8 - Regulation increases costs.

- Regulation does not automatically result in cost increases, any more than increased production volumes automatically result in lower costs. It depends. Regulation must address the root cause of problems, not perceived problems.

- There is a perception of increased costs with regulation, while ignoring where costs actually decrease as a result of regulation.

- The perception of increased costs is based on local or unit cost increases, while ignoring system-level or total costs.

- REAL Lean (flow) is a highly regulated environment, yet it has the lowest costs.

E9 - Economies of scale.

- Flow has little or no economies of scale because set-up time, queue time, and transportation time are small compared to batch-and-queue processing. Therefore, achieve flow and forget about economies of scale as a means of reducing unit costs.

- While scale may be needed to serve certain customers or markets, economies of scale may not actually exist even in batch-and-queue processing because executives ignore all diseconomies of scale.

- Diseconomies of scale that are often ignored include: expensive capital equipment and service contracts, large inventories, inventory management personnel, sales incentives, obsolete materials, commodity management teams, contracts personnel, auditing personnel, travel expenses, advertising, executive salaries, corporate office overhead costs, low productivity white collar workforce, delays and re-work, training costs, top-tier consultants, outside counsel, etc.

- If you ignore nighttime (costs associated with diseconomies of scale), then it is always daytime (savings associated with economies of scale). You are simply operating under a theory of ignorance.

- Serve your customers well by creating flow and do not worry about economies of scale.

E10 - Short-term financial focus.

- Having more-or-less exclusively short-term financial focus is an example of zero-sum thinking: The long-term is sacrificed for the short-term.

- When do you plan on going out of business? If the answer is never, then why have a strong short-term focus?

- You must do a better job of managing investors' expectations. You may also need to find inventors with a mid- to long-term focus.

- You should not provide earnings forecasts. Let the equity analysts do their homework.

E11 - Debt and leverage are good.
- Conservative businesspeople must be financially conservative. They should not be leveraged 30:1 or even 10:1.
- Debt is not good simply because debt financing is cheap and because interest is tax deductible.
- Increasing risk to the business's ability to withstand economic problems and bad management decisions - both of which will happen with 100 percent certainty - is not good. You must focus on long-term survival.

E12 - Outsourcing lowers costs.
- It depends. Unit costs are lowered only in calculations, driven by labor cost. Unit price reductions do not include total costs.
- Total costs are not taken into account because costs which accumulate in different budget categories are difficult to assign to specific items.
- Batch-and-queue processes outsourced to batch-and-queue producers (whether manufacturing or service) do not improve labor productivity or responsiveness to the marketplace.

E13 - Sellers' market view / supply-driven.
- Executives must match the production system (whether manufacturing or service) to market served.
- Using a sellers' market batch-and-queue production system when the company serves buyers' markets sets everyone in the company up to fail.
- Nearly every business process used today is a legacy of the early 1900s sellers' market (e.g. batch-and-queue, push material and information processing), when customers were willing to wait.
- You must change systems, policies, practices - as well as leadership beliefs, behaviors, and competencies - to reflect the actual buyers' market you serve.
- It is never smart to seek a sellers' market by controlling market

share, patents, etc. Doing this breeds complacency, and any advantages you have (patents, etc.) will eventually go away.
- Competition means to compete; not to sit back or enjoy having legitimately obtained, or gamed, a temporary advantage.

E14 - Batch-and-queue processing, standard cost accounting, and associated metrics.
- Executives must lead efforts to eliminate batch-and-queue processing in every process and, instead, achieve flow.
- They must lead efforts to use a cost accounting system compatible with flow.
- They must lead efforts to eliminate batch-and-queue metrics, or reduce the significance of batch-and-queue metrics, in decision-making.

E15 - Economic order quantities.
- Economic order quantities are consistent with a batch-and-queue sellers' market view, not a Lean demand-driven buyers' market view (see Appendix I and II).
- Economic order quantities assume change-over time is fixed and that customers can wait. Neither is true.
- Don't mistake equations and formulas for reality. Calculations may be true, but only "as far as that goes."
- You should produce what customers want, not produce according to what a calculation says is good for the company.

E16 - Fixation on unit costs and unit prices.
- Unit costs for goods produced and unit prices for purchased materials are important, but total costs and total prices are far more important.
- Executive decision-making will always be penny-wise, pound foolish when management is fixated on unit costs and unit prices.
- Time (chronomics) is a much more important measure, yet

management's attention is usually locked on unit costs (economics).

- Executives say: "Every cost element a company faces needs to be examined." Executives should instead say: "Every process a company uses needs to be examined." Costs are subordinate to processes.

E17 - Obsessive focus on labor cost.

- If workers are seen by executives as the problem, then labor cost can never be low enough. Free labor, it seems, would still cost too much. Labor cost is the wrong focus.
- Spending a lot of money on expensive technology to replace inexpensive labor does not make sense.
- It is more important to realize that people waste at least 50 percent of their time at work due to unclear expectations, lack of standardized work, etc. Full-time labor used only half of the time costs twice as much. Senior management owns that problem.
- Executives should focus on process costs, not labor costs.

E18 - Sharing is socialism.

- An outcome of customer satisfaction is wealth creation. Not sharing the wealth with workers and key business partners is zero-sum and inconsistent with the "Respect for People" principle.
- Executives want more money, and so do workers; both parties have something in common! Executives always find a way to reward themselves, why not also find a way to reward the people who actually create value that customers pay for?
- If workers improve productivity 50 percent, they must be rewarded for their efforts: higher pay (e.g. 10 percent) and cash bonus commensurate with the accomplishment. If suppliers suggest cost savings, then split the savings 50-50. If costs are lowered, prices for customers should be lower. Outcomes must be balanced.
- Socialism means a planned economy, equality, etc. Lean management is not socialism. It is concerned with fairness, but not

equality. Being stingy is not a defining characteristic of capitalism. There is no need to be stingy.
- Lean won't work properly without profit sharing.

E19 - Using suppliers as banks.
- Small suppliers are not your banks; their cost of capital is much greater than for a big company. Their weekly cash flow problem is real; yours is easily solved by commercial paper (when needed, unfortunately).
- Extending payment terms is zero-sum and therefore inconsistent with the "Respect for People" principle.
- Extending payment terms is not free: pay me now or pay me later. You are nuts if you don't think suppliers look for ways to get even - which increases your costs.
- Innovation and new product development are more productive than zero-sum financial engineering.

E20 - Cost is not real if it is not on a spreadsheet.
- Cost = measured cost + unmeasured cost. Unmeasured cost is always greater than zero. Just because some costs do not show up on a spreadsheet does not mean they do not exist.
- Unmeasured costs, or poorly measured costs, include rework, returns, conflict, etc. These exist due to poor processes, not because of bad accounting.
- Cross-functional work experiences and job rotations are important because they give people first-hand knowledge of unmeasured costs. They learn that these costs exist and do not need to see them on a spreadsheet to know they are real.

E21 - Budget cutting is cost cutting.
- Crossing out a line item on a spreadsheet and writing in a new, lower number is not cost cutting.
- Budget cutting tells people that process improvement is not

necessary in order to cut costs. Therefore, process improvement languishes. Costs remain because processes are unchanged.

- Budget cuts unilaterally reduce the price to do an activity, but not its costs.
- Focus on improving processes (e.g. cutting queue times), not budgets.

E22 - Precision is more important than relevance.

- The focus on obtaining precise numbers usually means that which is not precise or cannot be made precise is excluded from calculations. Thus, relevant information is ignored because it doesn't confirm the bias for needing precise data or information.
- Precision can take a long time and result in delays in decisions and making improvements.
- Kaizen teaches people when enough information has been obtained to be acted upon.

E23 - Continuous improvement is too slow.

- Continuous improvement seems slow only because improvement is occurring once in a while, versus daily, as it should be occurring if Lean management were understood and practiced correctly.
- Kaizen is a process for learning how to improve. This process must be repeated again and again to reinforce and expand the learning for all employees, including executives.
- Executives must allow learning to take place in the workplace (self and others) to avoid errors and future problems.
- Not allowing learning is inconsistent with the "Respect for "People" principle and places the burden of the business entirely upon management's shoulders. You set yourself up to fail.
- Big initiatives are difficult to execute and usually fail. You should always opt for daily improvement rather than big initiatives seeking home runs or quick hits.
- Gradualism is anti-Lean conservatism.

E24 - Must grow at double-digit rates.

• Rapid, double-digit growth is dangerous and generally not manageable.

• Growth becomes harder to achieve as the company's size increases. The demand for growth puts people in harm's way - i.e. getting blamed for not meeting targets that could not be met.

• Strive for stable long-term growth: 2-3 percent annual growth.

Key Point to Remember

Where are  *the Lean* *Economists?*

Microeconomics and some aspects of macroeconomics are based on a model of productive capability rooted in batch-and-queue material and information processing. With Lean management, you are striving to achieve flow in material and information processing. Therefore, many aspects of economics do not apply when flow exists (e.g. economies of scale).

Flow production has been in existence for over 100 years, yet, remarkably, economists still do not understand flow. They act as if flow does not exist and that batch-and-queue material and information processing is the singular and most appropriate productive model under all market conditions. Therefore, listen to economists at your own risk. They can easily ruin your company and your supply chains.

CAUTION

Economists and progressive Lean leaders have completely different views of standardization, productive capacity, machinery, scale, productivity, unit costs, efficiency, labor, customers, suppliers, investors, and communities.

2

Social Ideas That Must Diminish Or Be Eliminated

Business is a social science, which means it includes both human and economic dimensions. To reduce business to "the numbers," where everything and all decisions are seen as financial, is to simply grant yourself an amazing shortcut: to ignore the human dimension of business.

If a corporation's cash flow suddenly went to zero, or near zero, its executives would see this as a catastrophe. Yet, they have no problem inflicting this type of pain on employees who are laid off for non-emergency financial reasons. This is a common occurrence in large corporations under so-called "professional management," because the consequences of such zero-sum actions are far removed from executives.

The numbers are important, but business is not all about the numbers. If you do not like the social aspects of business, dealing with people and their problems, then you are in wrong job. As a leader, you must be curious to learn the true nature of problems. If you're incurious, then you are in wrong job. If you don't like serving others - employees, suppliers, customers, investors, or communities - then you are in the wrong job.

Flipping the business upside-down to turn what is fundamentally human into something that is inhuman is wrong. Business was created by people to satisfy both human and economic needs. The executives' role is not to unilaterally ignore responsibilities they dislike or find difficult to manage. Lean management requires executives to not take shortcuts and to accept their full responsibilities, not just the ones they like.

Read this chapter as follows: A brief statement labeled S1, S2, etc., represents an idea that is commonly held by executives, in thought or action. This is followed by short bullet points describing how the idea is inconsistent with Lean management.

***

S1 - People are the problem.

- Executives who think that people are the problem proclaim their ignorance of both process and cause-and-effect.
- You cannot be an effective leader of people if you think people are the problem.
- Executives must use the formal problem-solving processes that they have been trained to use, but never practice. People will rarely be the problem.

S2 - Blame people for errors.

- Blaming people cuts off the flow of information. You are guaranteed to get lots of unpleasant surprises.
- Poor information flow means the organization will not be able to respond quickly to changes.
- Blaming people is inconsistent with the "Respect for People" principle.
- Blame bad processes instead of good people. Executives must become much more process-focused to avoid blaming people.
- It is unwise and unjust to blame good people who are stuck in bad processes. Develop people's capabilities instead.
- Accountability must be accompanied with root cause analysis, not blame.
- Say "Thank you" to people when they make problems visible.

S3 - Manager ego, arrogance, and elitism.
- Ego, arrogance, and elitism put barriers between people and undercut teamwork.
- Separation of management from workers reduces the fidelity of information and blocks information flows.
- Ego, arrogance, and elitism almost always lead to bad decisions.

S4 - Individualism favored over teamwork.
- Executives exhort teamwork, but usually - and often unknowingly - favor individualism.
- Inconsistent messages cause confusion, which results in delays and inferior or inappropriate work.
- Executives who think that certain people are more important than others reinforce the view among workers that individualism is more valued than teamwork.
- Managers reward heroes who can temporarily intervene to correct bad processes. This undercuts teamwork. Improve the process instead of rewarding heroes.

S5 - Conflict has zero cost.
- Do not assume that because the cost of conflict does not show up on a spreadsheet that its cost is zero.
- Conflict causes time delays, re-work, etc.
- A lot of internal company conflict is inadvertent, driven by siloed metrics. These must be corrected in order to reduce or eliminate behavioral waste and achieve flow.
- Conflict compels stakeholders - especially employees, suppliers, and customers - to get even. And they surely will.

S6 - Process variation instead of standardization.
- Permitting wide variation, from the simple (not wearing safety glasses) to the complex (variation in business process from person-to-person or shift-to-shift), is a failure of management.

- Process variation exists, in part, because management does not correct the misperception that standardization means the "one best way." Standardized work means only "today's way," or, the current way to do the work.
- Standardize the work to set a baseline for improvement and to easily recognize problems so that problem solving processes can take place.
- Executives must be able to explain to workers why standardization is important, and that standardized work should be revised often.

S7 - Specialists stuck in their job.
- Managers tend to keep people stuck in the same job for the manager's own convenience.
- Keeping people stuck in the same job is inconsistent with the "Respect for People" principle.
- People stuck in the same job do not learn and cannot realize their full potential.
- Lack of job rotation and cross-functional work experience means that most people will continue to have a limited understanding of the company and its processes.

S8 - Layoffs due to process improvement.
- Executives who lay people off as a result of process improvement reveal a deeply embedded preference for short-term thinking and zero-sum outcomes.
- Layoffs kill continuous improvement, and also force management to pursue higher risk strategies for improvement, innovation, and growth.
- Laying people off due to process improvement is inconsistent with the "Respect for People" principle.

S9 – Introducing or perpetuating biases and stereotypes.
- Executives who think that certain colleges, majors, degrees,

functions, job titles, people, etc., are more important than others undercut teamwork.

- Thinking that engineering is more important than human resources, finance is more important than operations, or management is more important than labor, etc., initiates or perpetuates a dysfunctional leadership mindset. A company needs all functions in order to work properly.
- Perpetuating biases and stereotypes is not the function of management and is inconsistent with the "Respect for People" principle.

S10 - Business is a zero-sum "game" or "battle."
- Describing business as a "game" or as a "battle" are inappropriate metaphors because they create or reinforce zero-sum view of business.
- Business is not a game; people's lives depend on it.
- Business not a brute-force battle. Instead, use your brains and improve processes to better satisfy customers.

S11 - Workers serve leaders.
- Executives can expect low quality, highly interrupted information flows when their perspective is that workers serve leaders.
- Workers will live in fear and seek to avoid blame, which is inconsistent with the "Respect for People" principle.
- Leaders should serve workers because it results in improved information flows.
- Executives should say to workers: "Hello. Tell me your biggest problems," or, "Tell me the bad news first."

S12 - Leaders are smarter than followers.
- Rank is not a measure of intelligence, especially when promotion processes are usually political.
- Leaders know much less than they think because information is

highly filtered to deliver only good news.
- Arrogance is inconsistent with the "Respect for People" principle.

S13 - In-groups and out-groups.
- Favoring in-groups and diminishing the importance of out-groups leads to internal conflicts and blocked information flows.
- Favoring in-groups and ignoring out-groups is inconsistent with the "Respect for People" principle.
- Executives must take concrete actions to reduce any disparity between in-groups and out-groups.

S14 - Can be selfish and unfair.
- There is no business rule or requirement for executives to be selfish or unfair (zero-sum) to workers or other stakeholders.
- Management's decision to be selfish or unfair with any stakeholder is inconsistent with the "Respect for People" principle.

S15 - Disproportionate financial rewards for execs.
- Managers add no value to products or services.
- Big executive pay undercuts teamwork; it is prima facie evidence of selfishness and unfairness.
- Large pay disparities are inconsistent with the "Respect for People" principle.

S16 - Absence of profit-sharing.
- The absence of profit sharing demonstrates management's commitment to selfishness and unfair, zero-sum outcomes.
- Profit sharing creates a bigger pie, which leads to greater returns to investors.
- The absence of profit sharing is inconsistent with the "Respect for People" principle.
- Lean management will not work without profit sharing.

S17 - Ignore feedback from stakeholders.
- Stakeholders are like consultants; they tell you what's wrong and what to improve - and they do it for free!
- You must listen and respond to stakeholder feedback. The worse the news, the better. Thank them for their concerns.
- Ignoring feedback from stakeholders is inconsistent with the "Respect for People" principle.

S18 - Expansive say-do gap.
- Often there is a large gap between what executive say and what they actually do. Rank confers no right to be inconsistent and reveals a deep-seated zero-sum, us-versus-them, perspective.
- The say-do gap reflects a lack of self-awareness and a lack of leadership discipline.
- Not walking the talk undermines leaders' credibility.
- Say-do gaps are inconsistent with the "Respect for People" principle.

S19 - Static job description and promotion criteria.
- Job description and promotion criteria tend to be static over long periods of time. The process for changing both must be improved in a Lean business to support the daily application of Lean principles and practices.
- Jobs descriptions can be simplified to include the basic knowledge area(s), plus eliminate waste, unevenness, and unreasonableness using the scientific method.
- Promotion must be merit-based, not political, in Lean businesses.
- Capable Lean practitioners with good interpersonal skills are top candidates for advancement.

S20 - Wasteful leadership behaviors.
- Lean leadership behaviors are distinctly different from conventional management leadership behaviors.
- Executives cannot behave in a Lean company the same way they

behave in a conventionally managed company.
- Wasteful zero-sum leadership behaviors, typical of those found in a conventionally managed company, are inconsistent with the "Respect for People" principle.

S21 - Doing harm does no harm.
- Doing harm, unintentionally or otherwise, is not the job of leadership.
- Doing harm (layoffs, squeezing suppliers, etc.) is inconsistent with the "Respect for People" principle.

S22 - Respecting people is optional.
- The "Respect for People" principle is not optional in Lean management.
- People who are disrespected look elsewhere for whatever they need.
- Customers, employees, suppliers, investors, and communities will look to others for satisfaction.
- Lean leaders develop employees' capabilities and teach people how to apply problem-solving processes so that they can determine the causes of problems and identify practical countermeasures.
- Focus on process, experimentation and learning, versus results and answers.

Key Point to Remember

 Lean is Groovy

"Hey man, go back to your pad and dig this..."

CONTINUOUS IMPROVEMENT REQUIRES RESPECT FOR PEOPLE

RESPECT FOR PEOPLE REQUIRES HAVING A PROCESS FOCUS

HAVING A PROCESS FOCUS REQUIRES THINKING AND ANALYSIS

THINKING AND ANALYSIS REQUIRES ASKING WHY

ASKING WHY REQUIRES CURIOSITY

CURIOSITY REQUIRES HUMILITY

HUMILITY MEANS NOT THINKING YOU KNOW IT ALL

. . . .

This Is The Way Of Great Lean Leaders

Executives who think they know it all will establish a culture of dependence, where people are not allowed to think and cannot learn and improve. This is an example of disrespect for people. The great Lean leaders clearly understand they do not know it all. Therefore, they are able to more effectively decentralize problem recognition and problem-solving to reduce errors system-wide and improve responsiveness.

Lean management cannot function properly without the "Respect for People" principle.

3

Political Ideas That Must Diminish Or Be Eliminated

Any organization, be it a unit of just four people, or 400,000 people, has a propensity for politics to become part of daily work. Organizational politics can either be minimal and thus more-or-less inconsequential, or it can be stifling and lead to tremendous delays and incredibly bad decision-making that threatens the organization's existence. The more common case is for organizational politics to exist roughly in the middle of this spectrum, which damages the organization in small, sometimes imperceptible, ways over time.

Importantly, most people do not like organizational politics because they see it as waste - an activity and associated behaviors that adds cost and but does not add value. In addition, organizational politics creates unevenness and unreasonableness. Few executives ever bother to think about organizational politics in these terms, but they absolutely should. Then, they would realize that organizational politics, which is created by people, can also be eliminated by people.

Often, an organization's most talented people refuse to accept managerial responsibilities solely because of the politics they know they must contend with in the new role. Executives have a responsibility to ensure the right leaders are in the right positions at the right time. Organizational politics defeats that key responsibility.

So it is up to each member of the executive team to ensure the organization is as free of organizational politics as it can be at any point in time. Doing so will improve material and information flows, as well as responsiveness to changing business conditions.

*Read this chapter as follows: A brief statement labeled
P1, P2, etc., represents an idea that is commonly held
by executives, in thought or action. This is followed
by short bullet points describing how the idea is
inconsistent with Lean management.*

P1 - Company comes first.
- Executives often talk about the importance of customers - "customer is king" and "customer first" - but management decisions, processes, metrics, etc., indicate the company or its shareholders actually come first.
- Company-first or investor-first indicates a deep rooted unwillingness by executives to actually serve customers.
- This is an example of a large "say-do" gap that undermines management's credibility.
- The company doesn't create cash, customers do. The cash generators, the lifeline of the company, come first.
- Putting the company first or investors first is inconsistent with the "Respect for People" principle because it marginalizes the other key stakeholders.

P2 - Business principles are not needed.
- Most executives cannot articulate their business' principles. That means that almost anything goes. That's no good.
- A lack of business principles usually leads to destructive zero-sum management practices.
- Executives should adopt and apply the Caux Round Table *Principles for Responsible Business*.

P3 - Satisfaction with the current state.
- Current state value stream maps reveal management's satisfaction with current state.

- They also reveal that management is unaware of the value-creating processes and the material and information flow problems therein.
- Most managers do not look for problems. They think that having problems means they are not good managers.
- Managers with no problems have many more problems than managers with problems.

P4 - Power and bureaucracy as source of strength.

- The executive's position is actually one of great weakness because people will not tell them what is really going on.
- Bureaucracy is an excuse for not taking action and for staying comfortably distant from problems "on the floor."
- Despite talk of the need to change and to adapt, there is too much in place that supports the status quo.

P5 - Perpetuation of organizational politics.

- Organizational politics does not support businesses that serve competitive buyers' markets because it slows down and stops information flows and causes many unnecessary problems that usually never get fixed.
- Organizational politics is not a value-creating activity. It serves no customer, no investor, no worker, etc.
- Organizational politics is behavioral waste that executives typically tolerate and even encourage.
- The existence of organizational politics shows that executives are oblivious to a major problem and therefore do not use the problem recognition and problem-solving processes they were trained in.

P6 - Use of illogical and fallacious arguments to win.

- There is pervasive use of illogical arguments by managers, which results in delays and rework.
- People with bad news are turned away or made to be the loser.
- Winning by any means is inconsistent with the "Respect for

People" principle.
- Executives must be fact-based.

P7 - Zero-sum bargaining.
- Continuation of zero-sum, power-based bargaining routines ensures key stakeholders remain marginalized.
- The use of zero-sum bargaining shows that executives are oblivious to a major problem, and therefore do not use the problem recognition and problem-solving processes they were trained in.
- Executives must engage in joint problem-solving, as the parties involved share interests that are more similar than different.
- You learn more and improve faster with joint problem-solving that you do with bargaining.

P8 - One best way.
- Deep down, everyone wants to fix a problem once and be done with it, forever.
- This is inconsistent with the "Continuous Improvement" principle.
- It is also inconsistent with the "Respect for People" principle because things change over time.

P9 - Punish messengers for delivering bad news.
- Overtly or covertly punishing people for delivering bad news is a selfish, zero-sum reaction.
- Punishing the messenger shows that executives are oblivious to a major problem and therefore do not use the problem recognition and problem-solving processes they were trained in.
- Everyone, including executives, must practice a fundamental of business: apply the scientific method to problem solving.

P10 - Don't question authority.
- Executives' common view that they are right simply because they are in a leadership position is false. That is an illogical argument

(i.e. "false assumption," "abuse of expertise," and "expediency").
- The people who question authority, often indelicately, are simply trying to help authority avoid running aground. Say to them: "Thank you for caring."
- Leaders have to be able to take negative feedback from subordinates who question authority.

P11 - Blocked information and hiding problems.
- Blocked information and having to hide problems makes people unhappy and forces them to be deceitful.
- Many leaders believe it is more important to look good than to actually be good. This perspective adds risks to the business.
- Creating environments where information is blocked and where people must hide problems to survive is inconsistent with both the "Continuous Improvement" and "Respect for People" principles.

P12 - Technology improves processes.
- Cost-conscious executives often fail to understand the root causes of problems, and, instead, throw money at problems with the hope that technology will be the big fix.
- Technology may or may not be an appropriate solution, and is often used as a ruse to eliminate labor.
- Technology can cost much more than the labor needed to operate simpler processes.
- The application of technology must be consistent with the "Respect for People" principle.

P13 - Hard-wiring waste, unevenness, and unreasonableness (WUU).
- Modern enterprise software systems hard-wire waste, unevenness, and unreasonableness.
- Management unwittingly spends millions of dollars to become inflexible, which makes continuous improvement extremely difficult.

- People must not serve computer systems. Computer systems must serve people.

P14 - Political promotions.

- Most promotion processes are lengthy and time-consuming, and therefore contain lots of waste. This leads to shortcuts that diminish merit and emphasize politics. This, in turn, causes organizational unrest which undercuts teamwork.
- Promotions must be merit-based in a Lean organization. That means management must understand the job and become skilled at objectively comprehending merit.
- If Lean is important to an organization, then those who are promoted must be skilled in Lean management (both technical and behavioral).

P15 - Managerial self-interest.

- Managerial self-interest must be subordinated to customer interests.
- Lean management seeks servant leaders who put themselves last.
- Managerial self-interest is inconsistent with the "Respect for People" principle.

P16 - Unions, labor, suppliers, etc., are bad.

- Having a reflexive dislike of unions, government, labor, suppliers, etc., exposes irrational leadership beliefs, behaviors, and competencies that cut off flow of information.
- People in executive positions are expected to show greater management acumen, curiosity, willingness to listen, and balance.
- Key business stakeholders share interests that are far more similar than different.

P17 - Politics trumps scientific method.

- Executives engage in organizational politics to serve narrow personal interests. Politics does not serve customers and is waste.

- Executives must actively participate in the reduction and elimination of organizational politics.
- Instead of politics, executives must practice a fundamental of business: Apply the scientific method in problem solving.

P18 - Business is business.

- The phrase "business is business" is used by executives to justify and legitimize zero-sum actions.
- It is an excuse used to simplify business decision-making.
- Instead, business is human. It was created by people, for people.
- Business is human.

Key Point to Remember

FAKE LEAN

IS A LOSER

Executives mistakenly apply the same political thinking that they used for years in conventional management to Lean management practice. They do not recognize that organizational politics is a wasteful leadership behavior, because it adds cost and does not add value. It is a form of disrespect for people that quickly results in Fake Lean. Politics is greatly diminished or eliminated in a REAL Lean business because it impedes material and information flows.

The perpetuation of organizational politics by executives ruins Lean transformations.

4

History Reveals Repetition of Same Mistakes

You are in a management position because, in part, you want whatever happens to depend upon YOU. In fact, a lot of what happens does depend on you. Therefore, it is important for you to understand what has happened to people like you in earlier times. This will help you gain perspective and avoid making the same errors that they did.

Most executives think the times they live in are unique and that yesterday's problems have been solved and are no longer with us. They think today's problems are new problems worthy of their expertise. Not so. In most cases, today's problems are the same as yesterday's problems. By not studying management history or analyzing the major failures of companies such as Enron, Toyota, Xerox, General Motors, BP, etc., they never see what they could learn and apply to their job and to the business. It is irresponsible of executives to ignore the specific ways other businesses fail, both great and small.

History informs us of why it has been so difficult to advance Lean management, and for executives to correctly practice Lean management. Understanding the history of Lean management, including the issue of sustainability, will make you a more effective Lean leader. The result of that capability will be improved people, improved business processes, and improved business results.

As a manager of people and processes, you have a responsibility to understand the mistakes that others made before you, which, in many cases, led them or their companies to fail. You should want to know about that (see Appendix IV).

*Read this chapter as follows: A brief statement labeled
H1, H2, etc., represents a historical management
problem or error. This is followed by short bullet
points describing how the problem or error
detracts from Lean management success.*

H1 - Managers don't understand continuous improvement.

- Deep down, everyone wants to fix it once and be done with it. They seek the "one best way," which is inconsistent with the "Continuous Improvement" principle.
- The "one best way" is also inconsistent with the "Respect for People" principle because things are dynamic and change frequently.
- Managers must participate in continuous improvement. They must get out of the office daily to "go see," "ask why," and say "Thank you."

H2 - Managers ignore the "Respect for People" principle.

- Managers think they know what "Respect for People" means, or that they are already doing it - and doing it well. They are wrong.
- You cannot be Lean without this principle.
- Ignoring this principle increases business risk and greatly limits what can be achieved in Lean transformations.
- Executives must never forget that business is human; created by people, for people.

H3 - Managers stuck on zero-sum.

- Executives are stuck on zero-sum thinking because it appears to them to make their jobs easier.
- Zero-sum thinking undercuts teamwork within and between organizations.
- Preference for zero-sum thinking and outcomes is a self-imposed

management decision, not a law or requirement.
- Business must not be thought of and practiced as zero-sum.
- Lean management cannot be zero-sum, as this would be inconsistent with the "Respect for People" principle.

H4 - Managers do not engage in problem-solving.
- Most executives have been trained in problem-solving and formal root cause analysis, yet do not apply these to managerial problems.
- This is a major failure on the part of managers to learn and improve their own skills and capabilities.
- Workers copy what leaders do or don't do. Executives who do not do root cause analysis cannot expect workers to do root cause analysis.

H5 - Managers allow problems to linger.
- Executives have extraordinary patience with big problems and unreliable processes. They allow these to linger uncorrected for years.
- This is inconsistent with the "Continuous Improvement" and "Respect for People" principles.
- Problems are not recognized because executives are far removed from value-creating, cash-generating processes.
- All executives must periodically become personally engaged in kaizen, as team members, to correct problems and improve processes.

H6 - Managers prefer batch-and-queue material information processing and are unaware of flow.
- Executives are satisfied with stop-and-go material and information, and are unaware of flow.
- Batch-and-queue material and information processing gives a false sense of control.
- Executives talk "low cost," but, instead, support high cost batch-and-queue material and information processing.
- Batch-and-queue material and information processing requires

far less management knowledge, skills, and capabilities compared to flow.

H7 - Managers do not understand processes.

- Executives' understanding of what is going on in the business is usually vastly different than what is actually going on.
- Relying on people to tell you what is going on is a big mistake because most workers fear their boss. They will say "There are no problems," even though there are actually many problems.
- Executives must become personally engaged in kaizen, as team members, to understand and improve processes. Only then will they know what is really going on.
- Practice kaizen as if you were learning to play a musical instrument. Practice every day.

H8 - Managers are disengaged from daily improvement.

- Executives think: "I'm beyond that."
- It is not possible to ever be "beyond that" when it comes to business and business processes.
- Executives must become personally engaged in process improvement.
- Doing so will demonstrate to others your humility. It will show that you do not think you know it all, and that you are willing to learn.

H9 - Managers do not study and practice.

- Professional managers must study and practice the details of their profession for as long as they are managers.
- Like professional musicians, golfers, or artists, you must be immersed in studying and practicing your craft.
- Lean management requires daily application of Lean principles and practices.
- Organizational politics is not management practice. Deduct double the time you spend doing this from the time you spend practicing Lean management.

H10 - Managers focused on doing, to a fault.
- Most managers pride themselves on being "doers;" people who do things and who get things done.
- But "doing" all the time means little or no time for thinking. So, lots of things are done that do not need to be done, or are the wrong things to do.
- Lean requires executives to balance thinking and doing. Use the plan-do-check-act (PDCA) cycle.

H11 - Managers stop learning.
- Being an executive doesn't mean you are smarter than everyone else or that you can stop learning.
- Completing an undergraduate or graduate degree does not mean you are done with learning.
- Don't assume that getting A's in courses or being awarded a degree means that you know anything.
- What if what you have been taught has actually set you up to fail more than it has set you up to succeed?
- The workplace is full of interesting things to learn. Go to the workplace and learn.

H12 - Managers addicted to shortcuts, quick wins, and silver bullets.
- Don't take shortcuts.
- Professionalism is the result of unending practice and long-term adherence to fundamentals.
- Professional writers, musicians, golfers, etc., do not take shortcuts. Shortcuts make them less competitive.
- Reliance on shortcuts, quick wins, and silver bullets reveal a management that does not apply the formal problem-solving processes that they were trained in.
- If a quick win occasionally comes along, take it. But do not run the business based on seeking quick wins, or view your job as a

facilitator for quick wins.
- There are no silver bullets. Plan on hard work.

H13 - Managers focus on operations to cut costs.
- Waste, unevenness, and unreasonableness are in every business process, not just processes in operations.
- Executives must work towards synchronizing material and information flows across the enterprise.
- Focus on eliminating large differences in cycle times across all business processes.

H14 - Managers ignore key stakeholders.
- Most executives have great difficulty focusing on more than one stakeholder at a time.
- Many executives deny the existence of stakeholders, preferring instead to recognize only shareholders because doing so makes their job much easier. Keeping one thing constant among many variables appears to simplify the task of management.
- Executives fail to use stakeholders as resources. They do not understand their views or acknowledge their interests, and therefore make little effort to try to satisfy their interests.

H15 - Managers think: "We're different."
- Saying "we're different" is a common tactic used to maintain the status quo an avoid engaging in progressive management. It is usually accompanied by another delaying tactic: "Show me someone in our industry who has done this."
- You have mostly the same problems as any other business; they're just called different things or appear to be different.
- The actual level of uniqueness between businesses is perhaps 5 to 10 percent. They are typically 90 to 95 percent the same.
- At its core, Lean focuses on eliminating waste, unevenness, and unreasonableness, and problem-solving. Lean applies to any

business or organization.

H16 - Managers confuse tools and management system.
- Management tools are not the same as a management system.
- Most professors can't tell the difference either.
- Executives often fail to determine if a tool is consistent with business principles, management system, etc.
- They incorrectly assume universal application of tools to all management systems.

H17 - Managers fall for tools and cherry-pick tools.
- Executives have an insatiable appetite for tools in support of their unending desire for shortcuts and quick fixes to problems.
- That is why consultants focus on tools. There is a large and growing market of suckers who will overpay for tools that deliver quick wins.
- Management is the architect of business, not a tradesperson with a toolbox. A tradesperson's role is important but different from management.
- When presented with a new management system, executives invariably cherry-pick what they think are the good parts. They fail to see the interconnections between the tools and their relationship to the overall management system.
- Lean management is not a collection of tools for management to cherry pick from. To do so ruins Lean.

H18 - Managers inappropriately combine tools.
- Combining tools reflects the fact that managers do not think; they mostly just do.
- Many management tools are developed to solve problems that are unique to zero-sum conventional management and are not applicable to the non-zero-sum Lean management system.
- Executives must not blindly adopt tools. Doing so can easily create confusion and inconsistencies.

- Lean and six sigma are not compatible. The former seeks to make everyone a problem-solver, while the latter relies on specialists to solve problems. People delay problem solving when specialists are not available to work on their problem.
- Lean is simple and accessible to everyone, and six sigma is complex and accessible to only a few.

H19 - Managers beliefs, behaviors, and competencies remain unchanged over time.
- Executives think that leadership beliefs, behaviors, and competencies are uniform.
- Leadership beliefs, behaviors, and competencies are completely different for zero-sum conventional management than for non-zero-sum Lean management.
- Lean requires different leadership beliefs, behaviors, and competencies.

H20 - Managers ignore what does not fit with their views, desires, or commitments they have made.
- Everyone falls victim to confirmation biases. Knowing this, executives must be vigilant to avoid it.
- Executives should actively seek non-confirming views (e.g. this book) in a non-blaming and non-judgmental way.
- Flow, Lean accounting, Lean leadership beliefs, behaviors, and competencies, etc., do not fit executives' current state views. Therefore, they will likely ignore this book. It does not confirm their views or desires.

H21 - Managers repeat the same mistakes.
- Managers everywhere, throughout modern times (since ca. 1880s) have faced the same or very similar problems.
- Every manager thinks their situation is unique. It appears this way to them because they do not study business history. They think

their lives and times are different.

• You are not unique. You are one of millions of managers who have faced the same or very similar problems.

• Executives should study and analyze the failures in other businesses or organizations so that the same or similar thing does not happen to them or their business (see Appendix IV).

Key Point to Remember

The pioneers of progressive management - Frederick Taylor, Frank Woollard, and Taiichi Ohno - all of whom were corporate executives, understood the importance of people in achieving continuous improvement. People - employees, suppliers, customers, investors, and communities - who experience zero-sum outcomes as a result of improvement activities will quickly withdraw their support and no longer participate.

Your greatest challenge in Lean management will be to practice and deepen your understanding of the "Respect for People" principle.

Next Steps

Step 1 was to read and comprehend this book. If you can accept all or most of what you have read, then move on to Step 2.

- **Step 2** - Complete the workbook *Practical Lean Leadership: A Strategic Leadership Guide for Executives*. It presents innovative and proven approaches to understanding and practicing Lean leadership in an easy-to-follow workbook format. It links Lean principles and tools directly to leadership beliefs, behaviors, and competencies, and does so in new ways that connect to the realities of the workplace.

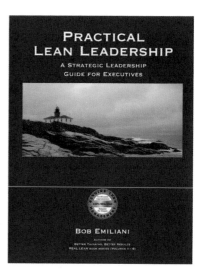

If you can accept and commit to practicing these new leadership beliefs, behaviors, and competencies, then go to Step 3.

- **Step 3** - Engage in policy deployment, shop and office kaizen, Lean accounting, etc. You can do this yourself. You should do this yourself. Leading change, at low cost, is your job.

The more likely outcome, unfortunately, is that you will hire one or more high-priced consultants to lead change in your organization. If you do this, be aware that consultants will, in most cases, be selling you Fake Lean. They will invariably be in the tradition of Charles Bedaux (1877-1944), narrowly focused "efficiency experts," selling you quick fixes that offer immediate cost savings - but little in the way of long-term success. You have to do that yourself. The big Lean consultants know exactly what you want to hear and how much you have to spend for Fake Lean. Can you resist their Siren song? If not, be careful, be selective, know the limits of the services you are purchasing, and don't just delegate work to Lean consultants - learn the details from them.

Continue your study and daily application of Lean principles and practices.

- **Step 4** - Read *Better Thinking, Better Results: Case Study and Analysis of an Enterprise-Wide Lean Transformation* and read *REAL LEAN* Volumes One through Six. *Better Thinking, Better Results* answers the question: "How do you conduct a total Lean transformation?" It is a detailed case study and analysis of The Wiremold Company's enterprise-wide Lean transformation from 1991-2001, notable for the integration of both the "Continuous Improvement" and
"Respect for People" principles. It is an authoritative and practical Lean implementation manual that helps guide senior managers on their journey.

The *REAL LEAN* series of books explains Lean management in ways that hundreds of other books do not. These original and creative works are written for hands-on Lean practitioners. Each volume is thoroughly researched and well documented, and provides an abundance of new information and perspectives to help ensure success with Lean management. They emphasize Lean as a management system and the "Respect for People" principle because both are usually missing from the practice of Lean management today.

- Step 5 - Continue your study and daily application of Lean principles and practices.

Read other important books on Lean management to deepen your understanding and for inspiration. Focus on authors such as: Norman Bodek, Pascal Dennis, Takahiro Fujimoto, Mark Graban, Satoshi Hino, Jim Huntzinger, Masaaki Imai, Dan Jones, Jeffrey Liker, Brian Maskell, Yasuhiro Monden, Taiichi Ohno, Mike Rother, Masaaki Sato, Art Smalley, and Jim Womack.

Lean people read to gain new knowledge, and then practice the new knowledge to learn.

Keep practicing every day, as if you were striving to become a professional musician.

Closing Thoughts

Hopefully you were able to make it to the end of this small book without vomiting. If so, then bravo! You have gained, perhaps reluctantly, a clear picture of how remarkably different Lean leaders' minds are compared to conventional leaders' minds. The differences range from great to small and reflect an overall way of thinking that completely upends the norm - for the customer, and for the better.

The question now is whether or not you will allow yourself to mentally evolve from where you are today to become a skilled Lean leader. Your thinking will not evolve by itself. You must personally engage in the application of Lean principles and practices to re-wire your brain to the more advanced, progressive ways of thinking that Lean embodies.

You have a rather simple choice: You can continue along with conventional management - i.e. zero-sum capitalism - and rationalize it as good enough. After all, everyone is doing it, why should you be any different? I think you should be different if you are a leader. Leaders lead change directed towards making positive progress and improving people's lives. If you are a leader, then advance your understanding and practice of business towards Lean management - i.e. non-zero-sum capitalism.

If you are an executive of a publicly-owned business, you have a large burden to grow the business, week by week, month by month, quarter by quarter, and year by year. The burden is so great that CEOs and CFOs will do almost anything to grow, even if it is very expensive, highly disruptive, and benefits only one stakeholder at the expense of all other stakeholders.

It seems that anything that does not contribute to growth is not funded. This includes wage growth. Workers have experienced flat or declining real wages over the last 30 years or more. Corporate growth at the expense of the middle class - the workers who actually create the value that customers pay for - is a flawed long-term strategy that has already inflicted great damage on our nation. Challenge yourself to grow together with your stakeholders, rather than growing apart from them.

If you are an executive of a privately-owned business, or a non-profit, growth may not be as important to you as profitability and cash in the bank. Lean management can help improve these and other internal and external measures of business performance. No matter what, the correct application of Lean management requires major adjustments to how you think about the economic, social, and political aspects of business, and a strong commitment to avoiding historical errors.

Lean management offers a lower risk approach to organic growth. The rate of growth may not be headline-grabbing double digits, but it will be healthy growth that employees and suppliers can reliably deliver and that investors will admire. But to achieve this, you have to accept what you have read in this book in its entirety - and more (see "Next Steps").

Success with REAL Lean requires a different understanding of economic, social, political, and historical aspects of business. If you can understand and accept these differences, then you will move forward faster in your Lean transformation because you will have started to remove the barriers that block material and information flows.

Finally, please recognize that you can also use this book to diagnose problems with your own Lean transformation (see Appendix III) and identify practical countermeasures. You can also use it to help identify causes of failures in other organizations (see Appendix IV). For example, Toyota Motor Corporation's auto recalls and other serious problems in 2009 and 2010 were caused by a regression to conventional management thinking among certain senior executives and their staff, beginning in the late-1990s in the following areas:

E3 - Companies exist to maximize shareholder value.
E7 - Free market fundamentalism.
E9 - Economies of scale.
E10 - Short-term financial focus.
E11 - Debt and leverage are good.
E13 - Sellers' market view / supply-driven.
E16 - Fixation on unit costs and unit prices.
E24 - Must grow at double-digit rates.

S2 - Blame people for errors.
S3 - Manager ego, arrogance, and elitism.
S9 - Introducing or perpetuating biases and stereotypes.
S12 - Leaders are smarter than followers.
S13 - In-groups and out-groups.
S17 - Ignore feedback from stakeholders.
S20 - Respecting people is optional.

P1 - Company comes first.
P4 - Power and bureaucracy as a source of strength.
P6 - Use of illogical and fallacious arguments to win.
P9 - Punish messengers for delivering bad news.
P10 - Don't question authority.
P11 - Blocked information and hiding problems.
P15 - Managerial self-interest.

H2 - Managers ignore the "Respect for People" principle.
H4 - Managers do not engage in problem-solving.
H5 - Managers allow problems to linger.
H20 - Managers ignore what does not fit with their views, desires, or commitments they have made.
H21- Managers repeat the same mistakes.

Each of these problems serves as a starting point for root cause analysis and the identification of practical countermeasures.

Key Point to Remember

The image above shows an illustration made by Julia when she was six years old (left side). The illustration of the girl drinking water on the right side was made by Julia at age fifteen. Is Julia a gifted artist? Certainly not. She practiced drawing daily for nine years to develop her capabilities to produce the image on the right.

Similarly, your current state management practice is like the image on the left. You need to apply Lean principles and practices daily for nine years to develop your management skills into something that, metaphorically, looks like the image in the right. If you apply Lean principles and practices daily, in whatever way, no matter how small, you will begin to develop the beliefs, behaviors, and competencies characteristic of Lean leaders.

Most people do not like to practice.

Appendix I - Lean and Keynes

When something needs to be done quickly in business, such as obtaining several manager's signatures for an important contract, or manufacturing a component to satisfy a critical part shortage, the queue times associated with the activity are almost completely eliminated. A contract that normally takes weeks to obtain several signatures is walked through the process and has all of its sign-offs within a few hours. Likewise, a manufactured component with a lead-time of 12 weeks is completed in just a couple of days because the part is moved immediately from one process to the next.

Thus, in an emergency, processes quickly change from producer-focused, supply-driven batch-and-queue to customer-focused, demand-driven flow. Queue times are driven to near zero. Yet when the emergency subsides, processes revert back to producer-focused, supply-driven batch-and-queue. Queue times soon return to previous levels. Why does this happen? It is because normal economic times allow waste (i.e. activities that add cost but do not add value). Normal economic times, and especially prosperous economic times, hide the costs of lengthy queue times.

Progressive business leaders think about this situation and ask: "If we can do things quickly in an emergency, why can't we do it that way all the time? After all, people are waiting." Progressives leaders, recognizing the opportunity to substantially improve internal and external customer satisfaction, move forward to improve all business processes by, among other things, reducing queue times. Their efforts greatly reduce costs, improve quality, and reduce lead-times: exactly the performance that all senior managers call for, but most cannot achieve.

A similar situation exists when severe financial problems emerge in a macro-economy. Government leaders take actions to get to the desired condition quickly, bypassing slow moving, long lead-time processes. They cannot tolerate queue times associated with supply-side economics to trickle down the benefits of tax cuts to business and the wealthy to the people while the financial crisis rages.

As a result, government leaders reluctantly accept policy solutions they would not support in normal times. And so it is that when the macroeconomic situation is bad enough, free market capitalists famously proclaim: "We are all Keynesians now." Suddenly, everyone can agree that the lengthy queue times associated with supply-side economics are not acceptable. But why is the elimination of queue time acceptable in a crisis and not in normal economic times? The productivity of money is obviously greatest when benefits are delivered directly to the people. Why, then, knowingly reduce the productivity of money in normal economic times by exposing it to the uncertain outcomes that result from long queue times.

If Keynesian economics is good in times of macroeconomic crisis, why aren't the fundamental ideas behind Keynesian economics good in normal macroeconomic times? And how does this relate to the micro-economic condition of a company as it cycles through periods of economic success and distress? Why allow normal economic times to sanction waste and crisis to prohibit waste? Who is in control here? The "invisible hand" or management? It better be management.

• • • • •

The *REAL LEAN* series of books illustrated, in various chapters, how progressive Lean management is more closely aligned with demand-driven Keynesian economics than classical and neo-classical supply-side economics. Keynesians prefer that government stimulate demand at the consumer-level to boost macroeconomic performance. Supply-siders, on the other hand, do not believe in demand-side stimulus to address macroeconomic underperformance. Instead, they prefer to stimulate supply through tax breaks to business, and therefore readily accept the lengthy queue times required for its limited benefits to trickle down to people.

A company's current state value stream map depicting batch-and-queue material and information processing represents a supply-driven microeconomic condition. This type of value stream map is scalable to a nation's macro-economy because over 95 percent of businesses process material and information using the batch-and-queue method (resulting in only about eight inventory turns for the entire United States economy). Hence, in aggregate, queue times are very long and value-creating processing time is short.

Current state stream maps depicting batch-and-queue information processing show a picture of high cost, low quality, long lead-times, and poor responsiveness to changes in customers wants and needs. Therefore, batch-and-queue, supply-driven microeconomics (and, by extension, macroeconomics) is viewed as inferior. This method of processing will eventually lead to financial distress.

Future state value stream maps depicting flow, or at least supermarket-controlled output (quasi-flow), is well-known to result in a system with lower cost, higher quality, shorter lead-times, and much greater responsiveness to changes in customers wants and needs. This is what progressive business leaders strive to achieve because it positions the company to better survive changing business conditions.

Take the example of Company A, a microeconomic entity, whose costs are high and is financially underperforming. Management, looking to reduce costs, can lobby government officials for stimulus - tax breaks, etc. It can also do things internally that are like a tax break. It can produce more goods or services (e.g. overproduce) to absorb overhead and lower unit costs of production. The well-known economies of scale curve illustrates the internal "tax break" available to managers if they increase production. Because diseconomies of scale are completely ignored (e.g. queue times are typically lengthened, not shortened), managers view as axiomatic that costs decrease as production increases.

Thus, it is in management's interest to be supply-driven, to overproduce, but surely at the expense of being further disconnected from actual marketplace demand. If every management team seeks the same internal "tax break," then no company actually gains any advantage. The market is simply flooded with products and services, which must be discounted in order to sell (an obvious diseconomy of scale, and one which is typically ignored by management).

Take the example of Company B, a microeconomic entity, whose costs are also high and is financially underperforming. Management, also looking to reduce costs, can lobby government officials for stimulus - tax breaks, etc. But instead management creates its own "stimulus," internally, by rapidly transitioning from batch-and-queue material and information processing to flow. Set-up, queue, and travel times are dramatically reduced. Rather than getting a small tax break from government, it instead creates a huge "tax break" for itself by becoming much better connected to actual marketplace demand. The economies of scale curve breaks down under conditions of flow, so no internal "tax break" is available to managers simply by increasing production.

Being more closely coupled to actual marketplace demand invariably results in benefits to customers - lower costs or greater value, shorter lead-times, higher quality, etc. - which leads to increased market share at the expense of supply-driven companies. Customers are much happier when material and information flows than when it is processed batch-and-queue.

• • • • •

Whether a country or a company, there is always some problem that needs to be addressed: slow growth, lack of cost competitiveness, high unemployment, global competition, lack of investment, etc.

Say the macro-economy is in deep recession. The Keynesians view is that government is the only entity with sufficient financial resources to stimulate the economy. For exactly the same reason, companies look to government for bailouts or tax breaks (both are really the same thing) in difficult economic times - and also when the economy is performing well.

Likewise, when a company, a micro-economy, is financially underperforming, the executive team is the only entity with sufficient managerial resources to supply progressive demand-driven management thinking to the company.

The question, always, is: Should supply (production) be stimulated or should demand (consumption) be stimulated to improve economic performance?

For the supply-side, who should receive the benefit of government's investment to ensure a vibrant macro-economy: business or the people? Clearly, the benefit should go to business, some of which may eventually reach consumers. Likewise, supply-side minded management will seek to ensure the benefit of overproduction goes to the company, some of which may eventually reach its customers.

Supply-Side Belief

Government Action	Company Action
Government gives money (tax cuts) to business.	Management overproduces to absorb overheads and reduce unit costs.

For the demand-side, who receives the benefit of government's investment to ensure a vibrant macro-economy: business or the people? Clearly, the benefit should go to the people, directly, with little or no queue time. Likewise, demand-side minded management will seek to ensure the benefit of flow goes to its customers, directly, with little or no queue time.

Demand-Side Belief

Government Action	Company Action
Government gives money to citizens/taxpayers.	Management improves processes to give cost, quality, and lead-time benefits to end-use customers.

It always makes sense to convert a micro-economy (a company) existing in competitive buyers' markets to become demand-driven. Queue time serves no purpose other than to consume resources without creating value. It also makes sense to convert a macro-economy (the nation) existing in a globally competitive buyers' market to become demand-driven, to reduce costs and eliminate the need for tax breaks (and government loans) to businesses. Indeed, the cost savings is so great that business can (and should) be taxed higher with no great ill effects. This is another example of how flow changes everything.

Remember, however, even micro-economies (companies) that are great examples of flow might be 95 percent demand-driven and still 5 percent supply-driven. While seeking to increase the proportion that is demand-driven, constraints in the real world may require some businesses to be partially supply driven, at least for a time. Yet, despite the wide-ranging benefits to all stakeholders of being demand-driven, the switch to from supply-driven to demand-driven macro- or micro-economies is never easy.

At the micro-economic level, everything that executives are taught about business in school and on-the-job reinforces both supply-side and supply-driven thinking and the appropriateness of long queue times. At the macro-economic level, there is a clear preference for supply-side economics among a majority of politicians in the U.S. Congress. Not only are they oblivious to the queue times associated with supply-side economics, supply-side economics (i.e. gifts to industry) helps them obtain financial support from business for election or re-election.

The recent U.S. Supreme Court decision in *Citizens United v Federal Election Commission* (21 January 2010), which permits unlimited corporate funding of independent political broadcasts, will further strengthen the relationship between business and government and likely entrench supply-side economics in macroeconomic policy for years to come. This can only serve to continuously reduce the competitiveness of the Unites States and of U.S. businesses. This outcome will not have been caused the "invisible hand."

If queue times are recognized, then it is simple to see how supply-side is a defective economic policy. It is, however, a highly effective political policy because it closely aligns the interests of elected officials and business, surely to both of their long-term detriment.

Supply-side politics is the price society pays when politicians and economists do not understand or care about queue time and its effect on people.

Appendix II - How Conservatism Fails Customers

The pervasiveness of Fake Lean, and of Fake Scientific Management generations ago, appears to prove that nearly every business leader possesses conservative ideology that retards empiricism and largely disables their ability to lead substantive change across the enterprise via process improvement. That, plus executives who are educated exclusively in batch-and-queue material and information processing, both formally and on-the-job, means that customer satisfaction will never be as good as it could be.

By saying "as good as it could be," I do not mean an ideal situation or occasional condition. Instead, I mean "as good as it could be" in an everyday sense. Customers expect much better focus on their needs from highly paid executives. Improvement that truly satisfies customers requires much greater changes than those that merely yield limited improvement rooted in gradualism and satisfies management's perception of low risk and control.

The most obvious example of ignoring empiricism is that business processes are almost invariably batch-and-queue, a method applicable if the market is a sellers' market, yet the actual market faced by most companies is a buyers' market. Customers have choices and do not like to wait. Therefore, material and information processing must not be batch-and-queue. The method must be flow.

The misfit between market (buyers') and management method (batch-and-queue) can only lead to slow decline, which most business leaders will have difficulty seeing. When they do, they often prescribe solutions that are regressive to try to capture past glories. Slow, regressive reform serves management's interests but not customers' interests. In some cases, improvements in productivity and efficiency are rapidly dismantled to regain power and control.

Modernizing ideas and methods to achieve flow requires executives to be far more progressive than they typically are. Many have been able to achieve some form of a hybrid batch-and-queue/Lean method of processing material and information (i.e. Fake Lean), but few have been willing to move beyond it. Process improvement takes energy. The classic routes to improvement are lethargic because they are informed by laissez-faire thinking.

Senior managers are very persistent. They try hard to create sellers' markets to gain advantages over their customers. Fake Lean is good enough for them because it adds to the bottom line without having to do too much different. However, having advantages over customers soon leads to complacency, and the only way to deal with the problems that complacency causes is through one simple zero-sum solution: aggressive budget cuts - e.g. lay people off, squeeze suppliers, close facilities, outsource or offshore work, etc.

These decisions reflect a far greater interest in policy than in day-to-day practice. Enterprise-wide productivity improvement, at the working level, is much less of interest to senior managers. Teamwork, whose importance is endlessly espoused, is unattractive to senior managers who prefer to do what they want to do, unfettered. You cannot expect teamwork if you do not model that behavior, or if the corporate political economy promotes selfish individualism.

Most executives have a strong preference for the "political method" over the "scientific method." This forces them into numerous decision-making traps and several forms of illogical thinking (see Appendix IV), which further distances them from problems - not to mention cash-generating processes. Failure to confront real problems enables batch-and-queue material and information processing to persist. This, in turn, generates many other types of problems that force senior managers to tell others what to do, and reduces workers to nothing more than unthinking manual labor. Self-interest, the retention of power, conflicts with the mutual interests of stakeholders. As expected, those who can see this problem and who call for change are usually marginalized. The "team" has lost a valuable member: one who can see reality.

The scientific method is a practical problem-solving process intended to be separate from political machinations. It is a process more closely associated with liberal thought than with conservative thought. Industrial conservatism makes it difficult to see real problems and understand their true cause(s), which increases risk. That should be incentive enough for any executive to want to see real problems.

Poor efficiency, in the eyes of conservative business leaders (and economic liberalism), is seen as correctable using simplistic solutions such as: increased competition (sometimes via oligopolies), new technologies, mass production, and economies of scale. Progressive economics views efficiency problems as more complex phenomena, whose solutions lie in dramatic product and process improvement - i.e. progressive reform.

Conservatism in business, while good for the boss, is bad for the customer. Conservative executives must be aggressively progressive in business, not wimpy progressive, to substantially improve customer satisfaction and to survive. Executives must, therefore, be educated for flow.

Appendix III - From Reading to Improving

The following pages contain examples of two simple spreadsheets that you can use to record ideas that you believed in before you read this book, compared to those ideas you now question or don't believe in after reading this book. This will pinpoint specific areas that you need to better understand or need more time to think about.

Each member of a management team can use these spreadsheets to input their views. The data can then be collected anonymously and plotted on radar charts. This will graphically illustrate areas of broad agreement and disagreement among the management team pertaining to key aspects of Lean management. It informs the management team of exactly what it needs to work on in order to make progress towards REAL Lean.

Examples of the radar charts for each category - economic, social, political, and historical aspects of Lean management - are shown following the two spreadsheets. The further the data points are from the center, the larger the discrepancy between how managers and Lean people think about the particular item.

These can be part of a broader action plan designed to move managers forward, from simply reading a book to gain new knowledge, to taking concrete action to learn and improve their understanding and practice of REAL Lean.

You can obtain the spreadsheets and radar charts shown on the following pages by sending an e-mail to bob@bobemiliani.com.

Agreement / Disagreement Spreadsheet

CATEGORY	BEFORE	AFTER
E1-Shareholder supremacy		
E2-Shareholder is the customer		
E3-Companies exist to maximize shareholder value		
E4-Rational self-interested maximizer		
E5-Invisible hand		
E6-Efficient markets		
E7-Free market fundamentalism		
E8-Regulation increases costs		
E9-Economies of scale		
E10-Short-term financial focus		
E11-Debt and leverage are good		
E12-Outsourcing lowers costs		
E13-Sellers' market view / supply-driven		
E14-B&Q processing, std cost acctg, and metrics		
E15-Economic order quantities		
E16-Fixation on unit costs and unit prices		
E17-Obsessive focus on labor cost		
E18-Sharing is socialism		
E19-Using suppliers as banks		
E20-Cost is not real if not on a spreadsheet		
E21-Budget cutting is cost cutting		
E22-Precision is more important than relevance		
E23-Continuous improvement is too slow		
E24-Must grow at double-digit rates		
E-Score		
S1-People are the problem		
S2-Blaming people for errors		
S3-Manager ego, arrogance, and elitism		
S4-Individualism favored over teamwork		
S5-Conflict has zero cost		
S6-Process variation instead of standardization		
S7-Specialists stuck in their job		
S8-Layoffs due to process improvement		
S9-Perpetuating biases and stereotypes		
S10-Business is a zero-sum "game" or "battle"		
S11-Workers serve leaders		
S12-Leaders are smarter than followers		
S13-In-groups and out-groups		
S14-Can be selfish and unfair		
S15-Disproportionate financial rewards for execs		
S16-Absence of profit-sharing		
S17-Ignore feedback from stakeholders		
S18-Expansive say-do gap		
S19-Static job description and promotion criteria		
S20-Wasteful leadership behaviors		
S21-Doing harm does no harm		
S22-Respecting people is optional		
S-Score		

Agreement / Disagreement Spreadsheet

CATEGORY	BEFORE	AFTER
P1-Company comes first		
P2-Business principles are not needed		
P3-Satisfaction with the current state		
P4-Power and bureaucracy as source of strength		
P5-Perpetuation of organizational politics		
P6-Use of illogical and fallacious arguments to win		
P7-Zero-sum bargaining		
P8-One best way		
P9-Punish messengers for bad news		
P10-Don't question authority		
P11-Blocked information and hiding problems		
P12-Technology improves processes		
P13-Hard-wiring WUU		
P14-Political promotions		
P15-Managerial self-interest		
P16-Unions, labor, suppliers, etc., are bad		
P17-Politics trumps scientific method		
P18-Business is business		
P-Score		
H1-Managers don't understand CI		
H2-Managers ignore the RP principle		
H3-Managers stuck on zero-sum		
H4-Managers do not engage in problem-solving		
H5-Managers allow problems to linger		
H6-Managers prefer B&Q and are unaware of flow		
H7-Managers do not understand processes		
H8-Managers are disengaged from daily improvement		
H9-Managers do not practice and study		
H10-Managers focused on doing, to a fault		
H11-Managers stop learning		
H12-Managers addicted to shortcuts & quick wins		
H13-Managers focus on operations to cut costs		
H14-Managers ignore key stakeholders		
H15-Managers think "We're different"		
H16-Managers confuse tools and mgmt system		
H17-Managers fall for tools and cherry-pick tools		
H18-Managers inappropriately combine tools		
H19-Managers BBCs remain unchanged over time		
H20-Managers ignore what does not fit with their views, desires, or commitments		
H21-Managers repeat the same mistakes		
H-Score		
TOTAL SCORE		

Economic

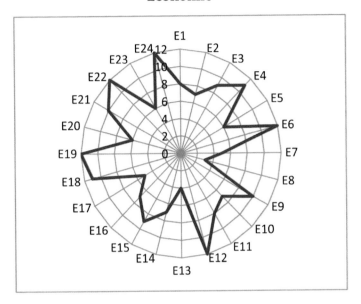

Social

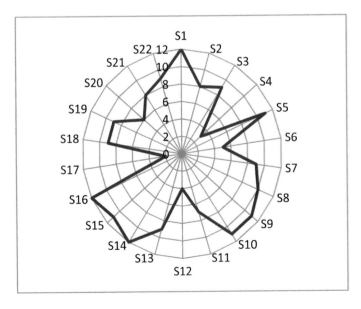

Political

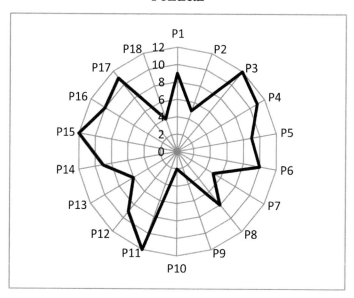

Historical

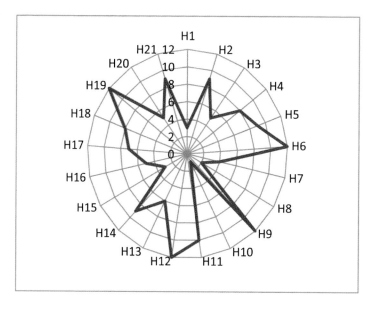

Appendix IV - Failure Analysis of Management Decisions

One of the most important duties executives have is to keep the business out of harm's way. They must avoid errors that cost great sums of money and damage brands and reputations. By errors and failures, I mean: cost, delivery, or quality problems; pitfalls related to rapid growth; problems in mergers or acquisitions; outsourcing failures; labor problems; recalls, etc.

Executives cannot successfully avoid or eliminate errors if they are unaware of their root causes. Therefore, it is critically important that senior managers develop the skill to analyze corporate errors and failures, even if the company under study is vastly different from their own in terms of size, number of employees, products or services offered, public or private, government or non-governmental organization, etc.

Do not fall prey to the mistaken view that what happened to a company or organization in a different industry or in a different country has no bearing on you or your company. In most cases, the root causes of failure are independent of the specific type of product or service.

Executives should be very interested in *any* type of major business error or failure because there is much to learn from and apply to their work. Typically, errors and failures made by others offer far more useful information to learn from than successes.

However, you will not be able to discern the actual causes of errors and failures simply by reading one story in the newspaper. You need to read many stories in the business press that describe the problems in chronological order. Then, you must analyze what you have read in an organized and systematic manner.

What follows is a practical process, tested and improved over more than six years, that you can use to analyze business errors and failures. Conducting business failure analyses on a regular basis, individually and as a management team, will greatly deepen your understanding of the causes of failure and help you identify and implement countermeasures that help ensure such problems do not occur in your business.

You will also learn, over time, the pattern of failure and similarities, which usually are many, and differences, which remarkably are few.

The steps to create and analyze business major errors and failures are as follows:

1. Collect stories on a company or organizational failure and arrange them in publication date sequence. The failure can be for any company in any industry. Sources for stories should be articles from *The Wall Street Journal*, *The New York Times* business section, *The Washington Post* business section, *Fortune*, *Financial Times*, etc. Save the articles as .pdf files or scan the paper copies into .pdf files.

2. Combine all the stories into a single .pdf file, oldest story first to newest story last. It should contain a minimum of 15 pages and a maximum of 125 pages.

3. Circulate the .pdf file to the senior executive team. Give them a deadline (usually one week) to read the file and analyze the failure using the Worksheets 1-4 shown on the following pages. This should be an individual assignment. To fill out the decision-making traps section of Worksheet 4, please read "The Hidden Traps in Decision Making," J. Hammond, R. Keeney, and H. Raiffa, *Harvard Business Review*, September-October 1998, Vol. 76, No. 5, pp. 47-58. To identify the illogical arguments section of Worksheet 4, please read

Being Logical: A Guide to Good Thinking, D.Q. McInerny, Random House, 2004, pp. 102-129.

4. Discuss the failure as a management team. This should include questions such as:

* Could this, or something very similar to this, happen to us? What would it look like?
* Is this currently happening to us?
* Are we so different that this could never happen to us? Couldn't the fundamental mode(s) of failure occur here?
* What would we do in such a situation? Are we prepared? Do we have a plan and know who would do what, when?

5. Circulate the .pdf file of the failure to mid-level managers and compare your failure analyses with theirs.

6. The senior management team should do at least two failure analyses per month. Each one will take 2 to 4 hours to complete. This activity should go on indefinitely, to continuously educate and train senior managers in how to recognize and avoid costly errors.

7. After completing several failure analyses, use the "Comparison of Failures" spreadsheet to compare and analyze the results. Take note of the ease with which senior managers succumb to basic decision-making traps, the extent of their use of illogical thinking, their level of overconfidence and certitude, and their lack of questioning. You should find this to be very humbling. Identify practical countermeasures to reduce or eliminate these causes of failures in your business.

8. After a year or so of analyzing the failures of others, begin to introduce failures that have occurred in your business. You will need

to pay a freelance newspaper reporter to interview people within and outside of the company and write a 15-50 page story about the failure. This will be the source material for the executive team's analysis. These failures must be analyzed objectively, even if the failure is a recent one that involved current leadership. Lean people don't blame or worry about who is at fault, they focus instead on improvement. If you cannot yet do this, then focus on analyzing the failures of other companies.

9. As you develop your capabilities to analyze failures, it should also improve your ability to predict failures. While nobody can predict the future, you should be able to identify recurring patterns that increase risk and could put you or your company on a path to failure. Read the business news for an emerging problem. Use the "Future Failure" worksheet (purple header) to analyze a failure that will likely occur in the future. Complete one of these per month. This activity should go on indefinitely, to continuously educate and train senior managers to understand how failures emerge over time.

Please don't say you do not have the time to do this. If you have the time to clean up the mess - which you always do - then you surely have the time to avoid it. Kaizen your schedule to make the time for failure analysis.

You can select any major error or failure currently in the business news. There is never any shortage of those. Or, you can gather electronically archived news stories of the failures listed below, dating from the late 1990s through the 2000s, to analyze in detail. For example:

A.I.G. Failure
Airbus A380 Development
BP Gulf Oil Spill

BP Texas Explosion
Blockbuster Video Bankruptcy
Boeing 787 Development
Baxter International's Heparin Blood Thinner
Big Pharma's Drug Pipeline Problem in the 2000s
Bristol-Myers Squibb Accounting Scandal
Catholic Church Pedophile Scandal
Coast Guard's Fast Response Cutter
Cost Management in Healthcare
Cost Management in Higher Education
Dell / Intel Accounting Scandal
Dell Faulty Computers
Egg Recall (salmonella)
Electricity Deregulation
Fall of Lehman Brothers, Merrill Lynch, etc.
General Motors Bankruptcy
Intel Chip Monopoly
Johnson & Johnson OTC Drug Recalls
Koninklijke Ahold N.V. Financial Scandal
Minerals Management Service Failed Oversight
Peanut Corp. of America Salmonella Recall
Pratt & Whitney PW 6000 commercial engine
Privatization of Public Assets
Public School System
Rite Aid Bankruptcy
Simmons Bedding Company
Sunbeam Bankruptcy
Toyota Late 2000s Quality Problems
U.S. Government Future Imagery Spy Satellite Program
U.S. Government Intelligence Failures
U.S. Great Recession, 2007-2010
Warnaco Bankruptcy

The executives involved in these failures were not uneducated or stupid. But, what if, instead of being educated on-the-job and in school to succeed, executives have actually been educated to fail? It would be wise to work off that assumption.

Please remember the following:

1) Do not think that what happened to a company or organization in a different industry is not relevant to your company. Any organizational failure, partial or complete, will provide you with extensive useful information you can act on, whatever business you are in. For example, BP's Gulf oil spill may seem irrelevant to you because you are in the cosmetics business. But, think again: The point of the BP failure was not spilled oil. It is that the worst that could happen did happen. What caused the oil spill will be similar to what might cause the worst to happen to your company.

2) Your root cause analyses may not be *exactly* right, and the countermeasure may not be *perfectly* effective. Do not be overly concerned about that. The point of doing root cause analysis is to improve your analysis skills, improve processes, and avoid repeat errors. You will be much better off than if you did not engage in failure analysis.

3) You must also focus on the process and not on the people. Failure analysis cannot become another means to blame people. Do not politicize failure analysis to achieve narrow personal or organizational interests.

As an officer of the company, it's your duty to understand how others fail and ensure that such outcomes do not occur in your company.

Tips for Completing Failure Analyses

- You do not have to read every word on every page. The articles will be redundant in many places because they represent a chronology of events and often repeat information that was presented in earlier articles.

- The most critical step is to understand what the problem is. There are usually one or two main problems and many smaller but related problems.

- Carefully scrutinize the conventional views and conventional wisdom expressed in the articles by the reporter or the people they quote when discussing the problem(s). These views may be on-target or could mislead you.

- Think about how your beliefs and untested assumptions relate to understanding the main problem(s). This may influence how you set up your 10 Whys root cause analysis.

- Since we are focusing on management (i.e. human) decisions, it is likely that your 10 Whys will sometimes focus on human factors - ones that are often related to common beliefs, untested assumptions, or behaviors.

- Think about these things as you read the cases:
  - It appears to be a problem in operations, but could the actual cause lie elsewhere (such as in finance, engineering, or sales and marketing).
  - What role did business metrics play in the decisions that were made?
  - What are the key decision-making criteria? Are they truly sound criteria?

- Was a "herd mentality" in play? Were managers simply following others? Why?
- Are there flaws in management's mindset that distorts the information they receive?
- Is management's perception of reality inaccurate? What's causing that?
- What does management do to preserve their inaccurate views of reality?
- Does management overestimate what they know or think they know?
- What personal attributes do top managers exhibit that block the flow of information or contribute to flawed views or decisions? What causes that?

• Don't fall for the common corporate excuses: lack of resources, no time, external factors, etc. These are not root causes. You must think more and dig deeper.

• If you get stuck, think about how you would respond if you were in that situation, and, what is driving your response. Ask: "Why would I do that?" Using yourself as an example will help. In most cases you are as smart and also educated in the same ways as the people who have made the error. In other words, we all fall into the same traps most of the time.

Tips for Completing Analyses of Future Failures

• The key to completing this analysis is to carefully scrutinize the mindset of management: their beliefs and untested assumptions, their decision-making traps, and types of illogical thinking. This is often best revealed in the parts of the articles where key people are quoted.

You can obtain the failure analysis forms shown on the following pages by sending an e-mail to bob@bobemiliani.com.

The Wisdom of Henry Ford

"A man who cannot think is not an educated man however many college degrees he may have acquired. Thinking is the hardest work any one can do – which is probably the reason why we have so few thinkers...

If education consisted in warning the young student away from some of the false theories on which men have tried to build, so that he may be saved the loss of the time in finding out by bitter experience, its good would be unquestioned. An education which consists of signposts indicating the failure and the fallacies of the past doubtless would be very useful.

...the best that education can do for a man is to... teach him how to think."

Henry Ford, *My Life and Work*, with S. Crowther, 1922, pp. 247, 248

This book has, in a small way, taught you how to think. Now you must commit to further study and practice to teach yourself how to think, and to teach others how to think.

Key Point to Remember

Don't Confuse Getting an A 🍎 or Receiving a Diploma 📜 With Knowing Anything

The positive feedback that successful people receive over decades of time, ranging from top grades in school to advanced degrees, to frequent promotions and raises, can easily make them think that they are very smart and know a lot. They become dangerously overconfident, and are usually unaware, and sometimes even immune, to the many warning signs.

People who understand Lean well reject these forms of feedback as evidence of knowledge - or as evidence of skill or capability as well. The attitude is one of humility, and of great awareness in that they do not know much more than they do know. And, what they do know may be correct only "as far as that goes."

Daily application of Lean principles and practices teaches executives, every day, that they have much more to learn. Most executives say they are life-long learners. Are you willing to prove it?

If you don't practice Lean, you don't learn Lean.

Instructions for Filling Out Failure Analysis Worksheets 1-4

Worksheet 1 - The purpose of this worksheet is to document the current condition. Typically, start on Worksheet 1, Box 1, but start elsewhere if that makes more sense to you.

- Please fill out your name, etc., at the top.
- Box #1 – Fill out as many items as you can to characterize what management was focused on (generally) immediately prior to the problem's emergence.
- Box #2 – Describe the current state upon the problem's emergence. List several items.
- Box #3 – List what managers did to address the problem.
- Box #4 – Identify inconsistencies between what management says compared to what it actually does.
- Box 5 – Identify beliefs or untested assumptions among managers that contributed to the problem. Please pay close attention to this and fill out as many items as you can.

Worksheet 3 - The purpose of this worksheet is to do your 10 whys analysis, show me your logic path, and to identify practical countermeasures.

- Follow the format given. Do not change it.
- List each question followed by the answer in italics as shown.
- Identify practical countermeasures where it makes sense to do so. You do not need to identify a countermeasure for each line item. Be judicious in your selection of countermeasures
- Identify at least two countermeasures.

Worksheet 2 - The purpose of this worksheet is to determine the dominant effect and to organize the causes into the categories shown.

- Identify the "Effect" in the top box. Use your judgment to determine the dominant effect. This will become the first "why" in your 10 Whys analysis.
- Identify and categorize the causes in each of the six boxes. In some cases, one or more boxes many be blank.
- Indicate the one cause category that you think is the biggest driver of the problem. Highlight the text in that category in **BOLD**.

Worksheet 4 - The purpose of this worksheet is to improve your knowledge and understanding of decision-making traps and, to improve your ability to identify illogical thinking, and to list the 5 key things that you learned in the case.

- Box 1 – Identify all major decision making traps.
- Box 2 – Identify all examples of illogical thinking. It can be illogical thinking exhibited by any party. Highlight the text in **BOLD**.
- Box 3 – List five key things you learned, in order of priority (first item = biggest learning). Please think carefully about what you learned from the case.

Follow these instructions carefully to learn the process for analyzing business failures.

| Name: | Assignment: | Date: | Worksheet 1 |

1. What issues did top managers appear to be most concerned about prior to the problems' emergence?

- Markets –
- Economy –
- Competition –
- Customers –
- Employees –
- Suppliers –
- Investors –
- Gov't regulator/regulation –
- Community –
- Themselves – (appearance, internal politics, etc.)

2. What is the current state (i.e. after the problem)?

3. What did the senior managers who owned the problem do to address these problem?

4. Identify at least three inconsistencies between what managers say and what they actually do.

5. Identify What beliefs or untested assumptions did company senior managers have that may have contributed to the problem(s)?

Worksheet 1: This page is designed to help you grasp the current situation and understand the real problem. Pay particularly close attention to boxes 4 and 5, as these are often principal factors in failures.

Cause-Effect Relationships

Worksheet 2a

EFFECT (This will become your first "Why?"):

Human . . . . .

Machine . . . . .

Methods . . . . .

Materials . . . . .

Measures . . . . .

Environment . . . . .

Indicate the One Cause Category That You Think is the Biggest Driver of the Problem (highlight text in BOLD)

Worksheet 2a: This is the classical representation of cause-effect relationships using the six cause categories historically found on fishbone diagrams. Use this or Worksheet 2b to document the effect and to populate the cause categories. Several items should be listed in most of the cause categories.

Worksheet 2b

Cause-Effect Relationships

EFFECT (This will become your first "Why?"):

HR Processes
• • • • •

Engineering / NPD Processes
• • • • •

Finance Processes
• • • • •

External (specify)
• • • • •

Sales & Marketing Processes
• • • • •

Operations / Supply Processes
• • • • •

Data / MIS Processes
• • • • •

Other (specify)
• • • • •

Indicate the One Cause Category That You Think is the Biggest Driver of the Problem (highlight text in BOLD)

Worksheet 2b: This is an alternate representation of cause-effect relationships using cause categories for the six key functional areas and their associated business process. This is intended to increase the focus on processes and problems caused by unstable processes in the major functional areas. Externalize as few causes as possible.

| 5 Whys / Countermeasures Worksheet (Remember, you don't have to stop at why #10) | Worksheet 3 |
10 Whys Analysis	Identify Two or More Practical Countermeasures to Help Realize a Desired State
1. Why.... - XyzXyzXyz...	
2. Why.... - XyzXyzXyz...	
3. Why.... - XyzXyzXyz...	
4. Why.... - XyzXyzXyz...	
5. Why.... - XyzXyzXyz...	
6. Why.... - XyzXyzXyz...	
7. Why.... - XyzXyzXyz...	
8. Why.... - XyzXyzXyz...	
9. Why.... - XyzXyzXyz...	
10. Why.... - XyzXyzXyz...	

Worksheet 3: Here we use the "10 Whys," rather than the "5 Whys." The reason is because most people stop at why #4 or why #5 when doing the "5 Whys" and therefore fail to discover the root cause.

Decision-Making Traps, Illogical Thinking, and Key Learnings Worksheet   **Worksheet 4**

1. Identify all major decision-making traps:

ANCHORING – Giving Disproportionate Weight to the First Information Received

STATUS-QUO – Preference for Solutions that Preserve the Current State

SUNK COST – Make Decisions that Support Past Decisions

CONFIRMING EVIDENCE – Seek Information that Supports Your Viewpoint

FRAMING – Making a Decision Based on How a Question or Problem is Framed

ESTIMATING/FORECASTING – Making Estimates or Forecasts for Uncertain Events.
Overconfidence – Believing our Estimates or Forecasts are Accurate. Prudence – Adjusting Estimates or Forecasts to "be on the safe side." Recallability – Predictions about the Future Based on Memory of Past Events.

2. Identify all examples of illogical thinking (highlight using underline):
• Denying the Antecedent: If A then B; Not A therefore, Not B.
• Affirming the Consequent: If A then B; B therefore, A.
• False Assumptions: Knowing or suspecting the assumption is false but using it anyway.
• Using and Abusing Tradition: Using tradition to argue against something.
• Ad hominem: Attack the person, not the argument.
• Avoiding the Force of Reason: Make false claims, obfuscate, mischaracterize, or use power to avoid confronting someone's argument.
• Abuse of Expertise: Using expertise or experts to justify an action.
• Red Herring: Divert someone's attention from the problem at hand.
• Inability to Prove Does not Disprove: Ask questions that emphasize minutiae or seek highly specific answers.
• False Dilemma: Persuading people there are only two choices when there are many.
• Special Pleading: Omitting key information because it would undermine my position.
• Expediency: Ignoring the means to achieve a desired end.

3. List five key things you learned in prioritized order (first being most important).
•
•
•
•
•

Worksheet 4: Decision-making traps and illogical thinking are major factors in failures. Carefully identify these and fill out as many as you can. Collect this data over time so that you can begin to identify the major recurring decision-making traps and forms of illogical thinking, and develop countermeasures.

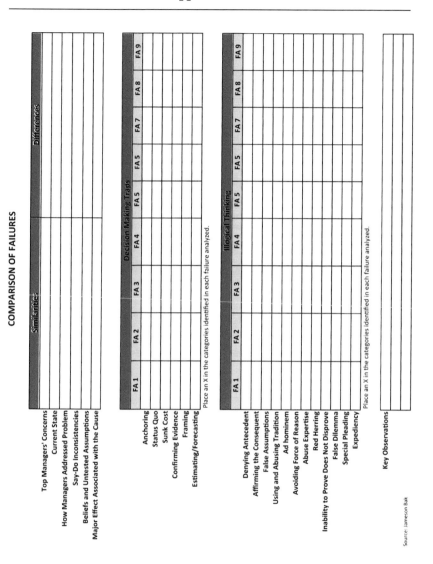

COMPARISON OF FAILURES

Comparing Failures: After completing several failure analyses, use this spreadsheet to compare and analyze the results. Take note of the ease with which senior managers succumb to basic decision-making traps, the extent of their use of illogical thinking, their level of overconfidence and certitude, and their lack of questioning. Identify practical countermeasures to reduce or eliminate these causes of failures in your business.

Name:	Future Failure:	Date:

1. What are the beliefs or untested assumptions?
-
-
-
-

2. Identify all major decision-making traps:

ANCHORING – Giving Disproportionate Weight to the First Information Received	•
STATUS-QUO – Preference for Solutions that Preserve the Current State	•
SUNK COST – Make Decisions that Support Past Decisions	•
CONFIRMING EVIDENCE – Seek Information that Supports Your Viewpoint	•
FRAMING – Making a Decision Based on How a Question or Problem is Framed	•
ESTIMATING/FORECASTING – Making Estimates or Forecasts for Uncertain Events. Overconfidence – Believing our Estimates or Forecasts are Accurate. Prudence – Adjusting Estimates or Forecasts to "be on the safe side." Recallability – Predictions about the Future Based on Memory of Past Events.	•

4. Identify all examples of illogical thinking (highlight using <u>underline</u>):
- Denying the Antecedent: If A then B; Not A therefore, Not B.
- Affirming the Consequent: If A then B; B therefore, A.
- False Assumptions: Knowing or suspecting the assumption is false but using it anyway.
- Using and Abusing Tradition: Using tradition to argue against something.
- Ad hominem: Attack the person, not the argument.
- Avoiding the Force of Reason: Make false claims, obfuscate, mischaracterize, or use power to avoid confronting someone's argument.
- Abuse of Expertise: Using expertise or experts to justify an action.
- Red Herring: Divert someone's attention from the problem at hand.
- Inability to Prove Does not Disprove: Ask questions that emphasize minutiae or seek highly specific answers.
- False Dilemma: Persuading people there are only two choices when there are many.
- Special Pleading: Omitting key information because it would undermine my position.
- Expediency: Ignoring the means to achieve a desired end.

4. What future failures do you think are likely to happen? List as many as you can think of, and be as specific as possible (better than 50/50 chance of occurrence).
-
-
-
-
-
-

Future Failures Worksheet: Use this one-page worksheet to analyze future failures.

About the Author

Please visit www.bobemiliani.com
to learn more about the author.

Feral Managers

The feral manager is one who has escaped from domestication and turned to a wild state. Feral managers disrupt business ecosystems and contribute to the extinction of key stakeholders such as employees and suppliers.

- Adapted from Wikipedia

The domestication process for young people is led by parents and K-12 teachers. They provide advice and counsel for 18 years to help children become responsible adults that contribute to society. Their teaching is unconditional, having no restrictions for circumstance, time, or place. No exceptions.

Parents and Teachers Say	What Many Managers Do*
"Be thankful."	Complain about: workers, unions, competition, markets, corporate tax rates, "Buy American," Washington, uncertainty, global free trade, regulation, customers, criticism, etc.
"Don't lie or mislead."	Have an enormous "say-do" gap; obfuscate; do not admit errors; sell defective products or services to customers; inflating earnings; hide debt; blame people for process problems; conduct do-nothing employee surveys.
"Don't cheat."	Take shortcuts: accounting gimmicks, insider trading, under-resource activities (which lead to cost, quality, and delivery problems), price fixing, bid rigging, channel stuffing, underpayment.
"Don't steal."	Stock options backdating; squeeze suppliers' profit margins; cut employee wages and benefits; elective layoffs; overcharge customers; extend payment terms to suppliers; require rebates from suppliers.

Parents and Teachers Say	What Many Managers Do*
"Help out; do your chores."	"Help out; do your chores." Forego cleaning up business processes; fail to meet often with employees and suppliers to get feedback and take action; procrastinate; ignore business process problems; disregard formal problem-solving processes; shun observation (to learn what is actually going on).
"Be fair."	Pay employees flat or declining wages; require employees to contribute more towards benefits; greatly increase executive pay; game the tax system; bribes; pay to play.
"Be honest; tell the truth."	Condone and foment organizational politics; looking competent more important than actually being competent; blame others for own failings; nonstop spin; conflicts of interest.
"Treat others the way you want to be treated."	Zero-sum treatment of key stakeholders; public dress-downs; expectations not clear; give insufficient or unspecific feedback; ignore employee or supplier suggestions; blame people for errors.
"Share with other people."	Reject profit-sharing for workers; withhold information and feedback; generally gain at someone else's expense (zero-sum view).
"Don't hurt anyone or anything."	Lay people off, close plants and offices, and squeeze suppliers; deficient in efforts to reduce environmental impact; covert or overt discrimination; ignore managerial incompetence; condone mentally or physically unsafe workplace.

* Particularly in large corporations. These are examples, not a comprehensive list.

Nobody is perfect and work is not neat and clean, but this is fucking ridiculous.

Moving Forward Faster can help in efforts to re-domesticate feral managers so they can return to society and become more valuable contributors.